Rethinking the Five Solae

Why *Messianic Judaism* Is Incompatible with the Five Foundations of Protestantism

Jacob Fronczak

Rethinking the Five Solae

Why *Messianic Judaism* Is Incompatible with the Five Foundations of Protestantism

Jacob Fronczak

Copyright © 2021 First Fruits of Zion. All rights reserved.
Publication rights First Fruits of Zion, Inc.
Details: ffoz.org/copyright

First Fruits of Zion is a 501(c)(3) registered nonprofit educational organization.

Printed in the United States of America

Publisher grants permission to reference short quotations (less than 400 words) in reviews, magazines, newspapers, web sites, or other publications in accordance with the citation standards at ffoz.org/copyright. Requests for permission to reproduce more than 400 words can be made at ffoz.org/contact.

ISBN: 978-1-941534-58-8

Unless otherwise noted, Scriptural quotations are from The Holy Bible, English Standard Version, copyright © 2001 by Crossway Bibles, a division of Good News Publishers. Used by permission. All rights reserved.

Cover design: Avner Wolff

Quantity discounts are available on bulk purchases of this book for educational, fundraising, or event purposes. Special versions or book excerpts to fit specific needs are available from First Fruits of Zion. For more information, contact ffoz.org/contact

First Fruits of Zion

Israel / United States / Canada

PO Box 649, Marshfield, Missouri 65706-0649 USA
Phone: (417) 468-2741   Web: ffoz.org

Comments and questions: ffoz.org/contact

LEARN MORE
ffoz.org

CONTENTS

Preface 1

Sola Scriptura, Part 1 5

Sola Scriptura, Part 2 23

Sola Fide, Part 1 45

Sola Fide, Part 2 59

Sola Gratia 81

Solus Christus 99

Soli Deo Gloria 123

Conclusion 131

Endnotes 137

PREFACE

Entrepreneur and bestselling author Seth Godin is famous for, among other things, claiming that "heretics are the new leaders. The ones who challenge the status quo, who get out in front of their tribes, who create movements ... they are the keys to our success."[1] In that vein, Godin invokes the example of Martin Luther, who famously nailed ninety-five theses to the church door in Wittenburg in defiance of the doctrine and practice of his generation's Roman Catholic Church.

While Godin's example might grate on Protestant ears, I am inclined to agree. In fact, I would say that no one is a heretic if not Luther. Like any other heretic, Luther was dissatisfied with the status quo and brave enough to do something about it. Like any other heretic, Luther was marginalized and attacked by those in power. But while most heretics in his day caught fire, Luther instead set one of his own. Thanks to Luther, the decades following him saw Europe ablaze with discontent, with rebellion—with heresy.

We still have Lutherans today, even though we don't often hear them called heretics. In the intervening centuries, thousands of leaders have followed Luther's example and started movements of their own; many of these men and women also escape the accusation of heresy.

Since Luther, Protestants have rewritten the rules that define heresy and orthodoxy. These rules no longer directly hinge on the dogma of Roman Catholicism, but they do indeed reflect a dogma all their own. Against this dogma I've nailed my own set of theses, and I expect the response will be just as impassioned as that which Luther personally experienced from the definers of orthodoxy in his time.

Luther's heresy was to strike at the heart of Roman Catholic dogma: the magisterium, the body of authoritative tradition that shapes the structure, doctrine, and practice of the Roman Catholic Church. Mine is to strike at Protestantism's own magisterium, the Five *Solae*.

Where I end up will not be as far from Protestantism as you might expect. In fact, I believe I land closer to the Reformers on certain issues than do many modern Protestants. There is, nevertheless, "a flaw in the heart of the crystal"[2] of Reformation theology. This flaw opened the door for Christian anti-Semitism to flourish in Europe, a door Luther and his contemporaries could have closed but didn't.

While many scholars in as many books have pointed out Luther's anti-Semitism, this piece of Luther's life and theology is usually glossed over as an unfortunate and isolated misstep, one that is almost universally forgiven among Protestants due to Luther's extraordinary effectiveness as—well, as a heretic, a movement-starter, a leader of the Reformation. Luther gave us our entire paradigm; surely we can overlook the sad chapter of his life during which hatred for the Jews began to find its way into his thinking and writing.

I have come to nearly the opposite conclusion. I see in the Five *Solae* themselves the root of Protestant anti-Semitism. From my point of view, these five statements, as they are normally understood, are designed to exclude Jews as much as Catholics from any definition of true and biblical religion. As the *Solae* persist, so this definition will persist; these fundamental statements simply leave no room for Jews or Judaism.

The aim of this book is to re-examine the Five *Solae* from a Messianic Jewish perspective. I believe that the paradigm these five statements represent, unless it can be radically redefined, is inimical to a truly Messianic Jewish theology and worldview. If you are a Christian of another stripe who has found your way to this book and you are unfamiliar with Messianic Judaism, you will almost certainly find this book provocative, but I am less certain that you will find it entirely useful. You may first want to take a look at my other work—the *Matters* series[3]—to get an idea of how I have arrived at a Messianic Jewish worldview and whether you would find that worldview as helpful to you as it has been to me.

So begins my admittedly quixotic undertaking—to be to Luther what Luther was, in his day, to Rome. I don't know whether I will succeed; history may prove me wrong and may, after all, remember me as a heretic. But like Luther himself said, "My conscience is captive to the Word of God ... To go against conscience is neither right nor safe. God help me. Amen."

CHAPTER ONE

SOLA SCRIPTURA PART 1

One of my seminary professors once challenged my belief in the sufficiency of Scripture, a Christian doctrine that states that the Bible is sufficient to answer all our questions about faith and practice. He was responding to a statement I made to the effect that neither Calvinism nor Arminianism—Christian theological systems designed to explain seemingly contradictory statements about predestination in the Bible—are to be found in the Bible's pages.

Apparently, according to this professor, one must be able to come to a conclusion in this area to live out his faith properly. He didn't say this outright, but there was no other reason for him to challenge my belief in the sufficiency of Scripture. Unfortunately, the class ended before we were able to continue the discussion.

The professor's challenge to me was based on a Protestant doctrine called *sola scriptura* (Latin for "by writings alone"). This doctrine, along with four others—*sola fide, sola gratia, solo Christo* (or *solus Christus*), and *soli Deo gloria*—formed the theological basis for the Protestant Reformation. All these doctrines have long and venerable histories, and today they remain the foundation of all Protestant thought. *Sola scriptura*, however, is the cornerstone, the one on which the rest depend.

Today, the popular understanding of *sola scriptura* encompasses several different concepts, including the Bible's "exclusive authority, infallibility, perspicuity, self-sufficiency, internal consistency, self-evident meaning, and universal applicability."[4]

To define *sola scriptura* without academic terminology might sound something like this: The Bible is the only *real* authority in the believer's life, and any others that exist must depend on it; it is never wrong about anything; it touches on every aspect of life; it needs no outside help to be correctly interpreted; it never disagrees with itself; it can be understood by anyone of average intelligence; and it applies to everyone in every situation.

The doctrine of *sola scriptura* was specifically designed to counter the Catholic belief that the authority of orally transmitted church traditions is equal to that of the written revelation, the Bible. To understand the Catholic view against which the Reformers fought, it will be helpful to read the *Catholic Encyclopedia*'s articulation of the basic concept of divine tradition from the article "Tradition and Living Magisterium":

> The Council [of Trent], as is evident, held that there are Divine traditions not contained in Holy Scripture, revelations made to the Apostles either orally by Jesus Christ or by the inspiration of the Holy Ghost and transmitted by the Apostles to the Church. Holy Scripture is therefore not the only theological source of the Revelation made by God to His Church. Side by side with Scripture there is tradition, side by side with the written revelation there is the oral revelation. This granted, it is impossible to be satisfied

with the Bible alone for the solution of all dogmatic questions.

> The Church, according to St. Paul's Epistle to Timothy, is the pillar and ground of truth; the Apostles and consequently their successors have the right to impose their doctrine; whosoever refuses to believe them shall be condemned, whosoever rejects anything is shipwrecked in the Faith. This authority is therefore infallible.

This Catholic belief has striking parallels with the belief in an inspired oral tradition held by many Orthodox Jews: There were oral traditions that were not initially written down; these traditions were transmitted accurately; the traditions are authoritative, and the traditions have divine sanction. Protestants, however, reject both Jewish and Catholic schools of tradition (both of which, of course, seriously contradict one another) in favor of the doctrine of *sola scriptura.*

It should be noted that originally (and it is still the case today in many circles), the doctrine of *sola scriptura* did not state that exegesis, exposition, deductive logic, and other skills are not necessary for apprehending the knowledge of Scripture. This indicates that one might need to appeal to a more learned authority who can better interpret the Scripture. However, it is also clearly understood in Protestantism that Scripture articulates doctrines in a clear enough way that its truth can be apprehended by a person of normal intelligence without the need for any oral tradition or external texts.

As beliefs go, *sola scriptura* is relatively new to the scene. Traditional Judaism and traditional pre-Reformation Christianity both held that traditions were necessary. A return to an authentic Apostolic-era Christianity, which finds its roots in Second Temple Judaism, entails the reconsideration of the importance of tradition and the validity of *sola scriptura*. I aim to show here that when a proponent of *sola scriptura* studies the Bible, he is relying on something other than the inspired Word of God, whether he realizes it or not. Furthermore, I seek to show that those who malign the investigation and examination of traditional Jewish literature to illuminate the text of the Scripture are themselves ignorant of their own reliance on tradition and the usefulness of extra-biblical literature.

> *If the Bible is the ultimate authority, the final source for all statements of faith and practice, it must state in the Bible that this belief is correct; otherwise, sola scriptura is a belief or tradition outside the Scripture that is also authoritative.*

Several examples best illustrate this: *Sola scriptura* itself (including issues of canonicity—that is, which books are included in Scripture), other creeds and statements of faith, translations of the Bible into other languages, extra-biblical literature, and rabbinic traditions (which could also be described as extra-biblical literature but are treated separately here). In moving through these five issues, we will move from conceptual problems with the doctrine of *sola scriptura* itself to practical issues that preclude our restricting ourselves to the scriptural text alone.

The first issue that comes to mind is this: If the doctrine of *sola scriptura* is true, then the doctrine of *sola scriptura* must be found in the Scripture. To state it another way: If the Bible is the ultimate authority, the final source for all statements of faith and practice, it must state in the Bible that this belief is correct; otherwise, *sola scriptura* is a belief or tradition outside the Scripture that is also authoritative.

We immediately run into a problem here, because the Bible doesn't refer to itself as such. Nowhere in the Bible does the term "Scripture" or any synonym refer to the entire work. It would be impossible for "Scripture" in the original context to have that meaning because the Bible is a collection of books by over forty different authors written over a long period of time. While the New Testament gives the Old Testament its stamp of approval, and Peter authenticates the writings of Paul, the acceptance of an earlier part is not conditional on acceptance of a later part (most obviously illustrated by the Jewish people, who accept the revelation of the Tanach but not that of the New Testament).

To put it simply, at some point one has to choose which books to accept and which do not belong in the Bible.

The question naturally arises: "Who decided which books were to be included in the Bible?" This question is currently quite popular, as evidenced by recent books and movies purporting to contain traditions that were arbitrarily left out of the Bible or suppressed by the church fathers. Catholics have an easy answer; they have no problem believing that the Holy Spirit revealed to the early church fathers which books were inspired (that is, breathed out by God through human authors) and which were not. However, Protestants have painted themselves into a corner here, as they reject any post-biblical tradition as authoritative.

Protestants tacitly accepted the belief that the canon was divinely ordained and that the tradition of canonization was outside the Scripture itself when they borrowed the Catholic canon entirely, not adding one single book to it (though the Apocrypha was later removed). However, Protestants do not believe that tradition itself is authoritative or infallible.

In settling the issue of canonization's status as a divinely sanctioned tradition, one of three possibilities is true:

- The Holy Spirit *did* reveal to the church fathers which books were inspired and which were not, and this tradition is infallible.

- The church fathers were able to discern which books were inspired through normal human means, and they were able to discern correctly, and this tradition is not to be called into question.

- The church fathers chose which books were inspired, and it is not known whether they chose correctly, and this tradition may be called into question.

Again, to state them a different way, there are only three choices: the canonicity of the scriptural books was *supernaturally revealed* to the fathers, was *discerned correctly* by the fathers, or was *incorrectly and artificially created* by the fathers. The Westminster Larger Catechism, a pillar of Reformed thought, states the following in response to the question "How doth it appear that the Scriptures are of the Word of God?":

> The Scriptures manifest themselves to be the Word of God, by their majesty and purity; by the consent of all the parts, and the scope of the whole, which is to give all glory to God; by their light and power to convince and convert sinners, to comfort and build up believers unto salvation: but the Spirit of God bearing witness by and with the Scriptures in the heart of man, is alone able fully to persuade it that they are the very Word of God.[5]

This answer is a sort of hybrid of the first two choices. That the books of the Bible comprise the Word of God should be self-evident; however, this truth cannot be fully apprehended without the aid of supernatural revelation. However, the Catechism skirts the concept of tradition entirely by implying that every Christian is the recipient of a supernatural revelation that the books of the Bible are inspired. That is, not only did the Spirit of God reveal to the early church fathers which books should be canonized, but the Spirit reveals to each believer today that the canon is correct.

Therefore, the doctrine of sola scriptura *itself, as practiced by many modern evangelicals, essentially holds the status of a divinely inspired oral tradition.*

This belief has its own problems. For example, how do we know that some inspired book was not lost and never rediscovered? How can Christians who never interact with extra-biblical literature conclude that it is not canonical? How do we respond to the fact that Christians have had disagreements over which books are to be included? Surely if each believer had a supernatural revelation as to which books were canonical, there never would have been disagreement. Martin Luther himself famously called the Epistle of James an "epistle of straw."

If the fathers of the Protestant church had to go through a process of debate and argumentation to decide which books were canonical, and these decisions are no longer allowed to be called into question, then it is a tradition and not a special revelation that continues today. Furthermore, belief in this tradition is required for members of modern Baptist and evangelical churches, as evidenced by countless "statements of faith" and by my own professor's great concern that I did not see his Calvinist doctrine in the pages of Scripture. Therefore, the doctrine of *sola scriptura* itself, as practiced by many modern evangelicals, essentially holds the status of a divinely inspired oral tradition.

In the same way, there are several other non-negotiable beliefs in modern evangelical Christianity (and, of course, every other branch of Christianity)—beliefs that are not clearly articulated in Scripture. The easiest example to deal with is the Trinity. Nowhere in the Scripture is the doctrine of the Trinity clearly articulated, and yet one would be hard-pressed to find a modern "statement of faith" that does not include it. In fact, in every Christian institution I have been involved with, whether academic or congregational, one would be excommunicated as a heretic for not believing in the Trinity. How did it come to be that so much importance is attached to a doctrine that is not articulated in any one place in Scripture?

Catholics, again, have an easy solution to this question. They simply believe that the tradition has been handed down accurately. But Protestants must find this doctrine in the Bible and still attach the great importance to it that Catholics do. As a consequence, several words can still be found today inserted into King James and New King James Bibles, in 1 John 5:7, that articulate the Trinity doctrine. However, without these verses (which are not present in any ancient manuscript), one must build this complex and mystical doctrine from various scattered references throughout the Bible.

How did the Trinity doctrine attain the level of importance and complexity it currently has? Surely if it were always a central doctrine, it would have been explicitly referred to in the Apostolic Writings. In reality, however, it does not emerge fully formed until after centuries of debate. Besides the sad fact that the church of the Nicene Era bore little resemblance to the sect of Judaism from which it developed, the question arises as to the eternal destiny of those who lived before the Trinity doctrine was fully articulated. Did they suffer eternal damnation because of their insufficient knowledge? If not, can we say that someone today is a heretic for not believing in the Trinity? Christians hold this doctrine to be so central and so distinctive that the phrase "the triune God" is often invoked as an unambiguous reference to the Christian deity (as opposed to the deity of another monotheistic religion—including, depending on who is doing the invoking, Judaism!).

I am not saying that I do not believe in the Trinity. What I am saying is that the doctrine of the Trinity attained its current level of complexity and importance as a result of traditions that have been passed down from the fourth century onward. It has essentially gained the status of a divine tradition within Protestantism. There are many other such traditions, a great number of which were simply carried over from Catholicism. Together they comprise a body of beliefs that Protestants unflinchingly adhere to while at the same time claiming that nothing besides the Scripture is authoritative for faith and practice.

Consider the ubiquitous "statement of faith" that must be agreed upon for one to enter a Christian college or become a member of many churches. If the Scriptures were truly the only authority and their teachings so clear that no confusion could arise as to their meaning, there would be no need for a statement of faith beyond "I believe that God has truthfully revealed himself in the Scriptures." Everything else would logically follow. However, the existence of this multitude of creeds and statements of faith is a testament to the fact that Protestants have placed certain traditions on the level of Scripture—that is, one must believe not only the Bible but also someone's specific interpretation of it to be considered Christian. This wouldn't be necessary if there were not multiple valid interpretations. Christian Smith calls this problem "pervasive interpretive pluralism" and considers it to be the death knell for *sola scriptura*.[6]

The third, and perhaps most obvious, issue with *sola scriptura* is that almost no Christians today actually read the Scriptures. By this, I mean that most Christians read and completely rely on translations, and these translations are not of the original manuscripts but of copies, which are themselves copies, and so on, back to the original manuscript. There is, therefore, a complete reliance on a textual tradition (that is, which texts are accurate copies and which are not) and on a translator. At first it may seem that I am nitpicking; however, one need look no further than the Masoretic Text itself to confirm this complete reliance on the traditions of others.

The Masoretic Text, from which every modern Old Testament is translated, consists of several parts. From top to bottom: first, on top of some letters there is a decorative flourish, or "crown."

Then come the letters themselves. After that, the *niqqudot*, "vowel points," which indicate the pronunciation of words. Finally, cantillation marks, much like musical notes, indicate how the text is to be sung.

> *By restricting their study to the English Bible,*
> *they introduce all the doctrinal presuppositions*
> *of the translator into their belief system.*

To those familiar with the original text of Scripture, this poses a problem: There were no vowel points in the original text. Hebrew students will be familiar with the truth that changing a few vowel points, or even placing the punctuation in a different place, can completely change the meaning of a verse. It can in some cases even be made to say its exact opposite. Consider this oft-used English example: "Let's eat, Grandma!" and "Let's eat Grandma!" are totally different sentences. Only the addition of a comma, one of the smallest and least significant punctuation marks, turns Grandma from a partaker to a meal.

The original text of the Old Testament contained no punctuation or vowels. The tradition as to which vowels are to be inserted is highly regarded within the translation community. I am not aware of any translation committee that completely discards the Masoretic textual tradition and supplies its own vowels. While they may make adjustments based on other texts, such as the Septuagint, for the most part, translators simply rely on the oral traditions of the Jews, transmitted now in a written form through the Masoretic vowel points, to tell them what a word means.

Even with the Masoretic traditions, however, many English readings of the Scripture can be divined from a single Hebrew text. Translation committees have to pick just one. Many times the readings that were chosen emphasize some Messianic prophecy that appears to point to Jesus Christ, while a Jewish translation committee might choose a different reading for the exact opposite reason. Both readings might be technically correct. However, doctrinal presuppositions dictate which reading is chosen. In effect, then, when Christians have only an English Bible and no other tools, they are completely unable to interact with the Scripture—the original Greek and Hebrew texts. They are completely dependent on the work of the translator.

To be fair, only a few Christians believe that the English Bible is inspired by God and sufficient for faith and practice. The vast majority believe that the Bible was inspired only in its original manuscripts and in its original languages. However, in a very practical sense, very few Christians make an effort to interact with the object of their veneration—the Hebrew and Greek Scriptures themselves. Even though they may believe that the original texts alone are inspired, they behave as if the English translation is enough. By restricting their study to the English Bible, they introduce all the doctrinal presuppositions of the translator into their belief system.

I am not saying that translations are bad. In fact, to obey Christ's command to preach the gospel to every creature, we are required to use translations. I met a missionary to Papua New Guinea who took eight years to teach the natives how to write their own language and to translate the Bible into their language to be able to present the gospel to them. How foolish he would have been to begin his ministry by teaching Hebrew, Greek, and Aramaic to the natives!

I use the example of translations only to illustrate the fact that in a very practical sense, the Scriptures in their original languages are, for most Christians, not enough—tools such as translations, concordances, the Masoretic vowel points, and commentaries are required to understand the text. Of course, the goal is to understand the original text, which in itself is not an objection to the doctrine of *sola scriptura*—until one realizes that every translation, every commentary, and *even the textual tradition itself* are all based on traditions along with the divine written revelation. It is simply impossible to get away from these traditions and to study the Bible in isolation.

The fourth issue is a completely practical one: the necessity of studying ancient extra-biblical literature. While many would agree that it is necessary to use modern tools to help interpret the Scripture, fewer are aware of the kind of light contemporary (that is, contemporary with the time period of the Scripture) texts shed on the Bible itself.

Some words and phrases in the Bible occur only once (or a few times) and have an unknown meaning, are not explained, or have a meaning impossible to discern from context. As Biblical Hebrew and *koine* Greek are both dead languages, this is a serious problem for a Bible student or translator. Many times a translator must guess at the meaning of a word based on a similar word or root.

Other times, however, the word appears in contemporary extra-biblical literature. How a word was used within the culture of the ancient world can sometimes be a total mystery until it is revealed in some other text. Consequently, the most recent lexicons will include uses of a Hebrew or Aramaic word in such texts as the Dead Sea Scrolls to flesh out the semantic range (range of possible meanings) of a word to find what it means when it is used in the Bible.

Extra-biblical literature can also shed light on practices, customs, and idioms that otherwise make no sense when they appear in the biblical text. The authors of Scripture assumed that their readers had a certain level of knowledge and acquaintance not only with the language they were using but with elements of the broader shared culture that are no longer necessarily known or practiced today. In some instances within the Bible, the author attempts to explain the broader cultural context of an event (Mark 7:3-4 is an excellent example). In most instances, however, the author assumes that the reader knows what he is talking about; otherwise, he wouldn't have bothered to write it. The authors of Scripture certainly didn't intend for the Bible to be as opaque as it seems to be today.

Why then do so many texts seem to prove so difficult for us to interpret today? It is because we are totally unfamiliar with the historical context. To discover the context and the idioms and practices of ancient cultures is impossible without extra-biblical literature, though sometimes the Bible itself can shed some light in this area. As the culture of the early church and the Old Testament authors was thoroughly Jewish, there is no more important extra-biblical literature than the large body of ancient Jewish literature that survives to this day, and specifically the rabbinic oral tradition.

The vast majority of Christians do not interact with the rabbinic tradition at all. As a consequence, the tradition is poorly understood and even attacked. Modern Jews have not forgotten the Christians who burned copies of the Talmud in Europe in the late Middle Ages. Even many in the Hebrew Roots movement disparage the teachings of the rabbis and ancient sages without realizing that in many ways we rely on these very teachings to interpret the Bible.

However, the influence of the rabbinic oral tradition is not limited to the Old Testament. Jesus himself frequently interacted with the oral tradition.

Possibly the most important way in which we rely on rabbinic tradition has already been discussed—the Masoretic Text. The Masoretes have handed the text of the Torah down to us; without them, we would not have had any Torah at all. The word "masorete" itself refers to this; it comes from the Hebrew *mesorah*, which is a reference to oral tradition. The preservation of the text cannot be separated from the community in which that text was preserved with all its traditions as to how the text was to be properly written and spoken. In effect, the entire Old Testament is dependent on this stream of tradition. This idea will have to wait for the next chapter of this book to be fully fleshed out.

However, the influence of the rabbinic oral tradition is not limited to the Old Testament. Jesus himself frequently interacted with the oral tradition. For example, in the Sermon on the Mount, he discusses adultery within the context of the contemporary debate between the students of Hillel and the students of Shammai. Beit Hillel said that a Jew may divorce his wife for nearly any reason. Beit Shammai said that a Jew could divorce his wife only in the case of marital infidelity. Jesus, in Matthew's account, simply sided with Shammai. He was not introducing a novel concept or disagreeing with the text of the Old Testament (which allows for divorce but does not specify in exactly what instance—hence the two disparate oral traditions). On the contrary, he was interacting with the oral tradition.

Incidentally, many times Jesus agreed with oral traditions that are still practiced today; for example, his teaching that the most important commandments are to love God with all one's heart, soul, and strength and to love one's neighbor as oneself is mirrored in the oral traditions and still widely accepted within Judaism.

Without the benefit of these oral traditions, many have seriously misinterpreted the Scripture. At one school I attended, it was taught that Jesus forbade divorce in every instance, except in cases where the marriage itself was already invalid (for instance, a homosexual marriage). While this interpretation is possible if one uses one specific definition of the Greek word *porneia*, knowledge of the rabbinic oral tradition would have precluded such an idea. This is one of many instances in which the text itself is insufficient without knowledge of the broader context (in this case, Jewish religious law based on oral traditions). The *sola scriptura* approach leads to *the wrong answer.*

If Jesus had no problem interacting with the rabbinic oral tradition, neither should we. After all, "It is enough for the disciple to be like his teacher" (Matthew 10:25). This does not mean that we need to regard the oral tradition as authoritative, but at the very least we must recognize that without it we risk a serious deficiency in our interpretation of Scripture.

These issues should be seriously considered by anyone who holds to the doctrine of *sola scriptura*, at least as it is commonly understood today. It is important to realize that traditions have played a huge role in bringing us to where we are. Even though the Bible is our authority for faith and practice, other writings have contributed immensely to making Christianity what it is, and in reality, many of the most central Protestant doctrines are the result of centuries of dialogue that were formulated into an authoritative body of tradition and not of strict exegesis of the Scripture.

While not all traditions are God-breathed or on the same level as Scripture, we must recognize the rich potential they offer in helping us understand the Bible. Protestants must begin to recognize that they, just like Catholics and Jews, have traditions that they consider to be authoritative. Also, we must realize that the study of extra-biblical literature is helpful and necessary to a proper understanding of Scripture and that understanding the rabbinic oral tradition can shed immense light not only on the Old Testament but the teachings of Jesus and the apostles as well.

Chapter Two

SOLA SCRIPTURA PART 2

In the last chapter we explored some fundamental problems with the doctrine of *sola scriptura* as it is commonly understood by modern Protestant Christians. "Bible Only-ism" simply doesn't work on a theoretical or a practical level, not only because the list of canonical books is a tradition created well after the formation of the faith, but because the Hebrew Scriptures themselves are the product of a body of Jewish tradition.

While many Christians claim to uphold *sola scriptura*, their traditional understandings of numerous important texts (many of them "proof texts" for particular doctrines) shape their theology and practice far beyond what the Bible explicitly teaches. Not only that, but there is no other alternative; the Bible simply doesn't address every situation or every matter of polity or even theology. There will always be room for interpretation, and the believing community will always have to supply that interpretation for everyone to be able to practice together. If the community doesn't supply an interpretation, strong-minded individuals will fill the gap with their own interpretations, and the subsequent controversy will provoke a schism. Our very own canon comes from just such a controversy—the one started by Marcion in the early formative years of the church.

The fact that different communities of faith have developed different and even opposing theologies and praxes is a testimony to this problem. Throughout the centuries, believers have had to repeatedly address issues on which the Bible is ambiguous or silent. Disagreements over the proposed answers to these questions have fractured denominations repeatedly. Some of the ancient liturgical denominations, such as Orthodoxy and Roman Catholicism, have remained relatively monolithic, or at least united. Protestantism, with its emphasis on *sola scriptura*, has suffered the opposite effect, with thousands of denominations having been created, each essentially claiming a monopoly on the correct interpretation of the Scriptures.

As the church moves into the postmodern era, it is becoming increasingly apparent to many Protestants that these divisions are not sustainable. Though this sentiment has existed in some circles since the 1800s and possibly earlier, it is even clearer now that Christians cannot afford to fight each other; they are no longer the dominant force in Western culture and therefore do not have the luxury or the resources to spend on infighting. Many Protestants are leaving their denominational churches for megachurches and other unaffiliated churches. Others are moving toward the Orthodox and Catholic churches because of these churches' long-term stability and traditions, which reflect a lengthy and meaningful history.

This, however, does not solve the problem. Abandoning recent streams of tradition for older ones may be a step in the right direction; however, the older streams of tradition are not without their issues. Two thousand years of continual development within the ancient liturgical churches have been sufficient to answer many unanswered questions; however, the revelations unearthed by modern critical scholarship—such as, for example, that Jesus was a practicing Jew and not a revolutionary out to start a new religion in competition with Judaism—cast doubt upon the answers that have been traditionally offered, and in turn, upon these ancient and venerable belief systems.

While many Christians may still be able to affirm with early church fathers such as Justin and Ignatius that Judaism is a relic of a bygone era—a stubbornly persistent error—the fact is that fewer and fewer Christians can conscientiously support this notion. It simply isn't supported by the New Testament (nor, of course, the Old). Not only that, but this idea paved the way for persecution and even wanton murder of Jews throughout the medieval period, something very few Christians today desire to remember, much less approve.

So what course should modern Christianity take? If *sola scriptura* has failed to produce a community that reflects the apostolic church, and the more ancient denominations have also failed (to whatever degree) to preserve the faith of our forebears within their traditions, is there a third option? Is there a way of interpreting and applying the Bible that will more reliably bring us to the place where we can emulate the first-century church established by the apostles, a place where we can be faithful to the teachings of Jesus and his first followers?

The Bible Inseparable from Community

The answer to this question hinges on the answer to an even broader one: What is the Bible?

Christians have historically relied on a purely theological answer to this question. To the Christian, the Bible is the revelation of God. It is, therefore, the most basic and essential standard for faith and practice. It represents God's will for his people.

They must begin to see the Bible also as a product and function of the community with which God maintains, and has historically maintained, a unique relationship—the Jewish people.

Modern historical-critical scholars, on the other hand, see the Bible as a historical document—or rather a collection of documents, a compiled record of the theological pontifications of a rather unique and prolific people—the Jews—as it finally found cohesive form in the Second Temple Period, having been gradually compiled and redacted throughout history by the spiritual leadership of the Jewish people in different times and circumstances.

Today nearly all serious academic encounters with the Bible are based on the historical-critical method—even those undertaken by believers. As a result, believing scholars must hold in tension the idea that the Bible they are studying is God's Word with the idea that the Bible is a very human document subject to layers of revision and editing by the community that initially produced it, thus finding its only authoritative interpretation within that community, the community to which the human authors and audiences belonged.

Following the polarization that occurred during the Fundamentalist-Modernist controversy, denominations that embraced the historical-critical method gradually tended to accept developments that would have been unacceptable to the apostles—for example, the solemnization of homosexual marriages. In contrast, fundamentalists continued to reject the historical-critical method; they instead read the Bible through the lens of traditional Christian doctrine.

As a result, many modern readers of the Bible fail to benefit, as believing scholars also do, from seeing the tension between the Bible as God's authoritative Word and the Bible as an inseparable part of the community that produced it. However, to move beyond the unworkable paradigm of *sola scriptura*, committed conservative Protestants must begin to see the Bible as more than a divine document that reflects God's inviolable testimony about himself and the world he created—not *less than* but *more than*. They must begin to see the Bible also as a product and function of the community with which God maintains, and has historically maintained, a unique relationship—the Jewish people.

I propose a conception of the Bible that mediates between these two ideas, one that will help us to see the Bible as God intends us to see it. I propose that the Bible is a window through which we grasp a greater reality: the person and work of God. In creating the Scriptures, God chose to work through the community of faith. Part of this work was to inspire the community to create a record of who God was (and is) and what he had done among them. The historical facts to which this record refers, rather than the text itself, are the faith-defining reality. The text is not an end in itself. Rather, it is a means—an inspired means but a means—to help the community understand God and itself.

Because of this, the text is the property of the community, and the tasks of interpretation and application properly belong to the community that produced it. In a way, the text is an extension of the community itself—a community memory—in addition to being a divine gift to the community.

There are distinct advantages to seeing the Bible in this way. First, it allows the believer to check his expectations of the text by the intention of the community—both the intent of the author and the intent of later interpreters from the same community (i.e., the New Testament authors' appropriation of Old Testament texts).

Second, it allows the community to respond in a united fashion to new problems through creative interpretation, allowing it to retain its literary heritage while also adapting successfully to new circumstances, all while remaining true to the intentions of the apostles and the spirit of their teaching.

Third, it gives the believer a strong hermeneutical foundation for maintaining the fundamental issues of morality and praxis—such as Jewish sexual mores—that have been abandoned by many mainline Protestant denominations.

Finally, it gives the believing community a strong epistemological basis by restoring it to the original intent of its founders, reconnecting it with its roots in Second Temple Judaism, and enabling it to interpret the New Testament in light of recent critical scholarship rather than relying purely on a traditional interpretive and doctrinal superstructure that may or may not allow the text to speak for itself.

The Community of the Text

The first question that must be settled is this: To what community does the text of the Bible belong? This is not an easy question to answer. Traditional Christian interpretation would offer the church—that is, the body of believers, or conversely, the institution of the church as legitimized by the apostolic authority of its leadership—as the answer to that question. So, both the Old and New Testaments are the property of Christianity and not of Judaism. An appeal in favor of this viewpoint might be made to 1 Corinthians 9:9-10 or Romans 15:4.

In this case, the traditional Christian exposition of the Scriptures would be canonized along with the Scriptures themselves, as the community to which the text belongs is the only community to whom the authority to interpret the text was given, and the multitude of other possible interpretations would simply be discarded. This is indeed the position of the Roman Catholic Church.

If it could be proven that the apostles were given *carte blanche* to reinterpret the Old Testament, which is inarguably the canon of the Jewish people and Judaism, as a fully Christian document with no further relevance to the Jewish people, this position would rest on rather firm ground. However, if the apostles interpreted the Old Testament fully within the bounds of what would be expected from the Judaism of that period, this would lead us to place the New Testament as well as the Old within the boundaries of Judaism.

While there are many works dedicated to the New Testament's use of the Old, Richard Longenecker's *Biblical Exegesis in the Apostolic Period*[7] is particularly useful here. Longenecker finds several particularly Jewish methods of interpretation used in the New Testament. Both *pesher*, which was a common interpretive method in the Qumran community, and midrash, which characterizes much of rabbinic interpretation, are freely used throughout the New Testament. While Longenecker hesitates to come to this conclusion, it seems clear that Jewish interpretive methods belie a fundamentally Jewish mindset and even an entrenched identity within Judaism on the part of the New Testament authors.

This is not to imply that, for example, Paul's epistles are somehow the exclusive property of modern Judaism. Paul wrote his epistles to predominantly Gentile Christian communities. However, as a growing number of scholars have postulated,[8] Paul himself belongs within Judaism, and so the "sending" community even of the most Gentile-oriented books in the New Testament is still completely Jewish.[9] So when seeking to interpret the epistles, certainly the Greco-Roman world of the *recipients* must be taken into account. Primarily, however, the *author*'s worldview is that of Judaism, even if Hellenized to some degree. His goal, ostensibly, is to draw his audience into his worldview; we should then seek to interpret the epistles as well through the lens of the Judaism of the Second Temple Period.

Two Communities

Within the context of this argument, the Old Testament presents a different problem than the New. The books of the New Testament were written and received within early Christianity. While the New Testament often reflects the tension between Jews who did and did not believe in Yeshua, it also primarily reflects a Second Temple Jewish mindset. Therefore, the believing

Second Temple Jewish community is the only community whose interpretation of the text is relevant to our study. The Old Testament, however, was written for Jews of an earlier period and then appropriated later by Jews of the late Second Temple Period and afterward—both those who believed in Yeshua and those who did not.

While the Jewish people have been happy to disclaim the New Testament, both Christians and Jews claim to be the legitimate spiritual descendants of Abraham and the Israelites of the Old Testament period. Both claim to be the rightful heirs of the Old Testament. And yet both Judaism and Christianity interpret the Old Testament outside its original context. Neither body of interpretation adheres to a strictly literal interpretation of the text; rather, in each faith tradition, the books of the Old Testament are woven into a canonical narrative that supports and affirms the identity and calling of the group that constructed the narrative. In Jewish tradition, for example, King Solomon is a great Torah scholar; in the Christian tradition, he is a tragic demonstration of the failure of the human monarchy to live up to the ideals of the Davidic covenant (and therefore a sign that the covenant spoke explicitly of Jesus).

Solomon's function as a historical figure in the narrative does not necessarily imply either of the above interpretations. These interpretations arose out of a desire to appropriate the Old Testament to the religious climate of Rabbinic Judaism and Christianity, respectively, and to anchor the faith traditions that produced them in the historical reality of God's interactions with the Israelite people—a reality accepted by both traditions.

So today's community of faith must reckon with not one but two interpretations of the Old Testament: that of the community to which its volumes were originally addressed and that of the first-century community that appropriated those texts to define and inform its own history, its future, and its current relationship with God. These two communities, though they were fundamentally connected, experienced the text of the Old Testament differently.

The New Testament was written by the God-ordained leaders of the Yeshua-believing community and is, therefore, a binding authority for that community.

Beyond the Text

This means that in reading the Old Testament, one may come upon passages that have more than one interpretation. Common sense and the historical-critical method dictate that the original meaning of the passage in its ancient historical setting is the primary import of the passage.

The tradition handed down from the apostles demands that we also regard their appropriation of the passage as valid. This is *not* solely because the apostles' interpretation of the Old Testament appears in the New Testament and is therefore "canonized." As Yeshua's agents, the apostles had the power to make these kinds of interpretive decisions for the believing community. Whether they had written them down or not, their interpretations would still be valid and meaningful for the community of faith. The authority of the New Testament derives from Yeshua and the apostles. It was written by the God-ordained leaders of the Yeshua-believing community and is, therefore, a binding authority for that community. It does not claim to provide an authority unto itself; it is authoritative because its authors had authority.

The apostles did not interpret the Old Testament in a vacuum either. Their interpretations often coincide with and even draw from other Jewish sources—non-canonical sources. For example, the book of Jude references *1 Enoch*, the *Testament of Moses*, and several oral Jewish traditions.[10] From the way Jude cites these works, it is apparent that his community not only knew of them but regarded them as reliable. At the point in history in which Jude wrote, the believing community apparently regarded these other works as important sources—again, not because of their inherent "canonized" status (they had none) but because they were products of the Jewish community and therefore relevant and meaningful to the people of God. These works helped the Jewish people tell their story and define their place in the world and their relationship with God. They hold this in common with the Scriptures. Both groups of literature are windows to a greater reality—the reality of God's relationship with the community of faith.

The Gospels provide a suitable analogy. Imagine sitting at the feet of Yeshua, hanging on his every word. As the Word made flesh, Yeshua spoke the very words of God. Truly hearing him in person would qualify as a direct revelation from God himself. Today we read the Gospel accounts, which provide a translated record of the words Yeshua spoke. According to the doctrine of *sola scriptura*, the Gospels are valuable because they are inspired by God—because he supernaturally directed the authors. I believe that this is correct, but it is not the primary reason we value the Gospels. The early church prized the Gospels because they recorded the words of Yeshua. The Gospels are a means to an end, and the end is to encounter and understand the revelation God gave through his Son.

This is, of course, not to say that the Gospels are not inspired; I believe that they are. It is merely to say that they are not the object of faith or the final reality of faith. They are a window through which we see a greater reality—the reality of the person of Yeshua the Messiah.

In the same way, the Old Testament is a means to an end. Certainly, it is inspired by God. However, the text itself is not the final reality or the object of our faith. It is a catalyst to help the reader apprehend the reality of God's relationship with Israel. The story of Abraham isn't valuable merely because it was written down in the Bible. On the contrary, it was written down in the Bible because it was and is valuable to the community of faith. We must keep ourselves from failing to make this essential distinction.

CHECKING OUR INTERPRETATION

Why is it so helpful to view the text as an extension of the community that produced it, a window to a greater reality, and not as an end unto itself? For one, we know more about the first-century community than the text explicitly tells us. For example, we know Paul was a Pharisee, but we don't know much about the Pharisees from the New Testament. We can learn more about Pharisaic beliefs—and therefore Paul's beliefs and background—from Josephus, who also wrote about the Pharisees.

Later works, too, can shed light on the state of Judaism in the first century—works such as the Mishnah, *Tosefta*, and the early Midrashim. And while scholars debate the usefulness of later works such as the *Midrash Rabbah* and the Talmud for this purpose, these works sometimes comment on Jewish life in the time of Jesus as well.

With a more robust, historically informed idea of what the first-century believing community probably looked like, we can get a better idea of what the authors of the New Testament texts meant. This is especially important when we encounter deeply meaningful Christian terms such as "church" and "gospel," which are so prominent in the New Testament but which appear to be nearly absent in the Old. The presumed lack of background for these terms has given interpreters nearly free rein for many centuries to develop complex ideas about exactly what these words signify. However, understanding how these terms would have been understood in first-century Judea and the Jewish Diaspora allows us to check these interpretations by inserting them into the first-century community and seeing if they make sense.

Toby Janicki's *Messiah Magazine* article "The Good News" provides a case in point.[11] The commonly understood Christian gospel message is that Jesus died for the sins of the world so that people can go to heaven when they die. However, Jesus preached the gospel during his lifetime (Matthew 4:23; Mark 1:14; Luke 20:1). His disciples were confused and alarmed in the days immediately preceding his passion when he began to speak of his coming death; when it happened, they were disappointed, disillusioned, and scattered. Surely he had not spent the previous three years preaching the popular Christian gospel of penal substitutionary atonement.

Therefore, when we encounter the term "gospel" in the New Testament, we must see it not in light of modern codifications or medieval church councils. Rather, we must see it in light of the Old Testament and particularly the writings of the Prophet Isaiah, who spoke repeatedly of the coming "good news," a gospel of hope for the Jewish people: the ingathering of the exiles, the restoration of the monarchy, and the Messiah shining a light to the nations. Moving beyond the *sola scriptura* approach, we must also consider how Isaiah's terminology was understood by the Second Temple Jewish community, as reflected in part by which passages were chosen for the *haftarot* as well as the appropriation of Isaiah by other Jewish literature.

> *But once we have found that "gospel" couldn't have such a meaning in the first century, we are obliged to reconcile our beliefs with the Scripture.*

Later interpretations of the term "gospel," in a non-chiliast Christian environment that held that the Davidic monarchy was never to be restored and that the Jewish people were forever to be scattered remove the particularly Jewish flavor from the term and make it relevant only to those who believe in Jesus. The result has been a gospel message no more complex than "Jesus died for your sins." But once we have found that "gospel" couldn't have such a meaning in the first century, we are obliged to reconcile our beliefs with the Scripture.

In this way, by adjusting our interpretations of key passages to reflect what the human author probably intended and what his audience would have understood, we can avoid a multitude of hermeneutical errors. This is not possible to do using only the Bible. In fact, the more extra-biblical literature we can get our hands on, the better we will understand the community that produced the Bible, and the better we will be able to understand the Bible itself.

Unified Creative Interpretation

Is it permitted for a Jew to drive a car on the Sabbath? Certainly driving a car doesn't qualify as "work" in the normal meaning of the English word. However, Orthodox Jews do not drive on the Sabbath.

How do they justify such a rule? The Bible, after all, doesn't mention cars. Not even once!

Orthodox Jewry has had to decide, with every new advance in technology, whether it is permissible to make use of each new invention on the Sabbath. Electric lights may not be turned on or off on the Sabbath. Computers may not be used on the Sabbath. These rules came about through creative interpretation of the Torah. These interpretations may not make sense to those outside the Orthodox Jewish community, but within the context of that community, they make perfect sense because they were born from that community and designed for that community. More than that, they help the community stay together by directing everyone to follow the same rules.

The collective interpretations that the faith community produces over the years gradually become authoritative and are codified in a body of tradition. In the Catholic Church, this body of tradition is called the magisterium; in the Jewish faith, it is the *torah shebe'al peh* (the Oral Torah). The idea of a tradition that is essentially mandatory for the community of faith is the very idea that *sola scriptura* was designed to counter. However, the community of faith still needs to develop new interpretations of Scripture to address new situations and concerns.

If the church is to remain united, then at some level it needs a unifying tradition with some degree of authority.

If these interpretations are not given some authoritative status in the community, the community will begin to split apart over disagreements—even petty disagreements. The fractured Protestant church is evidence enough of that. If the church is to remain united, then at some level it needs a unifying tradition with some degree of authority. Having no tradition whatsoever is simply not an option. Something has to fill in the blank when the Bible doesn't specifically address a certain situation. Either an earlier tradition is followed, or a new one is created.

But what happens when, as we discussed above, the tradition gets it wrong? After all, Martin Luther was right when he complained that Catholic priests in his day were withholding half the Eucharist—the wine—from the laity. This tradition flouted the clear instructions of Scripture.

The simple answer lies at the heart of the name of the Protestant Reformation. It was indeed intended to *reform* the very church from which it eventually split. And behold—today, Catholics all over the world drink from the cup of the Eucharist. The tradition changed. Reform happened. History shows us that while it may take many years for the community of faith to address its mistakes, it can and does do so.

The Catholic Church has been the most progressive denomination of Christianity when it comes to Jewish-Christian relations. It was the first denomination to officially repudiate supersessionism, which it officially did in the proclamation *Nostra Aetate*. Several recent popes have made great efforts to be friends of the Jewish people. While the Catholic Church has made mistakes in the past, it has been able to correct many of them, and the Second Vatican Council demonstrated the power of the magisterium to direct hundreds of millions of Catholics to abandon supersessionism and anti-Judaism. There is no way to effect that kind of positive change in Protestantism on anywhere near that scale.

When the tradition is wrong, clear-minded and Spirit-filled members of the community can advocate change. They can push for reform. The battle might be hard and even (as it was in the sixteenth century) bloody, but in the end, church traditions can be changed, and the community's leadership can set the church back on the right course.

Remember the Prophet Elijah's complaint to God: "I have been very jealous for the LORD, the God of hosts. For the people of Israel have forsaken your covenant, thrown down your altars, and killed your prophets with the sword, and I, even I only, am left, and they seek my life, to take it away" (1 Kings 19:14). God responded to Elijah that there were thousands of faithful Israelites.

These Israelites did not leave Israel. They did not go off and form their own community. They remained in the community of faith even as its leadership went off track. Eventually, the community reformed, and the perspective of the faithful won out over that of the idolaters in Israel. It was difficult and required patience, but in the end, Elijah's witness and that of his compatriots were used by God to effect change in Israel.

This is certainly not to say that all Christians should join the Roman Catholic Church. However, it is to say that leaving an established denomination due to disagreement is not *always* the best option. It is also to say that Messianic Judaism need not shy away from the process of slowly but deliberately building a resilient tradition of its own based on the traditions of the Jewish people and a heavily informed Jewish reading of the New Testament.

Remaining True to the Faith

One of the saddest results of the Protestant Reformation has been the wholesale abandonment by many major denominations of some of the most basic of the Bible's teachings. Several major Protestant denominations now accept homosexual behavior as normative. They solemnize homosexual marriages and ordain practicing homosexual clergy. This is in clear distinction to the Jewish sexual mores embraced by the early church, which in turn were based directly on the Torah.

The Protestant churches that have abandoned these foundational ideas of sexual purity and holiness can do so only because they have completely forgotten their Jewish roots. Not surprisingly, these denominations also tend to have a negative theological stance toward the Jewish people. They also often stand against the nation of Israel, not recognizing God's promise of that land to Jacob's descendants.

These unfortunate developments are the direct result of a *sola scriptura* mindset. How can I say this? Because when interpreters have only the Bible and not the Jewish context in which the Bible was written or an understanding of the community that produced the text, they feel free to choose one of many possible interpretations of biblical texts. Given the option, they have often chosen an interpretation that gives them license to do something that is prohibited.

When Paul writes against homosexuality, he uses an uncommon Greek word with a number of possible meanings. Interpreters in several mainline Protestant denominations feel free to choose a meaning that does not imply that homosexual activity is wrong. Instead, they argue that Paul is referring to the act of taking advantage of a young boy. Consensual homosexual activity doesn't hurt anyone, they reason, so there is no reason to forbid it.

The community that produced the New Testament, however, had a completely Jewish outlook regarding sexual mores. As Robert Jewett has rightly observed, Paul's deprecation of homosexuality was simply a function of his adherence to the Torah.[12] Understanding and yielding to the community of the text yield a correct interpretation; *sola scriptura* leaves the door open for interpreters to derive any number of meanings from the text, effectively rendering it useless for deciding these kinds of issues.

A Firm Foundation

Finally, seeing the text as an extension of the community rather than a conduit of information directly from God gives the Christian faith a firm foundation in Second Temple Judaism. The believing community that eventually grew into full-fledged Christianity was established by a sect of Jews who had seen their lives changed by the teachings of Yeshua of Nazareth. The New Testament is a record of this community's exploits, struggles, difficult decisions, and victories. But there is a difference between trying to live by the New Testament and becoming part of the community that produced it.

To embrace the text and not the community of faith is to put the cart before the horse. I realize that this is a dangerous thing to say of the Word of God; however, the Bible's significance as the Word of God is relevant only so far as it serves to connect the community of faith with God himself.

Because God's Spirit indwells the community of faith, the community embodies the reality of God's presence and work in the world. The purpose of the Scripture is to give definition and instruction to that community. Without the information recorded in the text, the community could not exist. However, without the community of faith, the text is powerless.

The text of the Scripture can be compared to software and the body of faith to hardware. It doesn't matter how much data you have if you don't have a computer to decode and display it. The Bible does not fulfill its function if it is nothing more than a closed book on a shelf or a historical document to be analyzed or a list of rules or a collection of stories. It is useful only when the community of faith appropriates it, when the community uses it to reconnect itself to the events recorded in the text and to the community that produced the text—and, consequently, to the God who founded the community through the events recorded in the text.

The modern community of faith stands on firm ground only so far as it maintains these connections. The text itself does not maintain these connections for the community; it is a critical and non-negotiable part of this maintenance process, but it does not replace the process. To be able to call itself a New Testament church, the church must have more than the New Testament. It must read the New Testament as the church and appropriate the text with the intention of connecting itself to the community that produced it.

> *It must read the New Testament as the church and appropriate the text with the intention of connecting itself to the community that produced it.*

This is all to say that one must let the vision of the apostolic community guide his interpretation of the text. If he reads the text without seeing it through the lens of that apostolic vision, he is bound to fall into error. While some may debate exactly what the apostolic vision looked like, modern scholarship has made it clear that it was very Jewish in character.

The realization of what this vision was has been realized only through implementation of the historical-critical method and through the abandonment of a purely *sola scriptura* mindset. The essential Jewish character of the text and of the community that produced it was not realized until interpreters moved beyond the text itself and began to analyze the social situation of the authors and audiences of the text.

The details may be argued for centuries to come, but the big picture the New Testament presents is a Jewish picture in which Jews and Gentiles work together to spread the gospel of the kingdom of heaven and the coming of the King of the Jews, Yeshua. The community of faith must appropriate this picture and begin to use it to define itself rather than relying on a *sola scriptura* approach or on church traditions that were developed without reference to this overarching vision.

Chapter Three

SOLA FIDE PART 1

The second of the Five *Solae*—five foundational concepts in Protestant theology that were developed to distinguish early Protestantism from Roman Catholicism—is *sola fide*. Latin for "by faith alone," *sola fide* is probably best known as the conceptual basis for the evangelical Christian gospel message: Sinners can be justified (i.e., saved) *by faith alone* in the atoning death of Jesus Christ. This is to be understood in contradistinction to the contemporary Roman Catholic doctrine of justification, perhaps best illustrated by the Catholic response to *sola fide*:

> If anyone saith, that the justice received is not preserved and also increased before God through good works; but that the said works are merely the fruits and signs of Justification obtained, but not a cause of the increase thereof; let him be anathema.[13]

> If anyone saith, that the good works of one that is justified are in such manner the gifts of God, as that they are not also the good merits of him that is justified; or, that the said justified, by the good works which he performs through the grace of God and the merit of Jesus Christ, whose living member

he is, does not truly merit increase of grace, eternal life, and the attainment of that eternal life—if so be, however, that he depart in grace—and also an increase of glory; let him be anathema.[14]

The Catholic Church has traditionally taught, in accordance with the above-quoted Council of Trent, that while the "first impulse" of the process of justification is an act of supernatural divine grace, "absolutely independent of man's merits," it is also deemed possible that one can resist the grace of God and prevent his own justification by refusing to undertake active "charity and good works."[15] Protestants were condemned at the Council of Trent for departing from this position and for teaching that justification is a work of God appropriated for the believer by faith alone and that it does not require any human cooperation whatsoever.

Protestant pioneer Martin Luther's well-known and oft-repeated epiphany, which he reportedly received after slowly and painfully climbing the Scala Sancta on his knees, had to do with this very issue—whether it was necessary for him to undertake such efforts in order to be sure of his salvation or whether his faith alone was sufficient to justify him before God.

Luther went on to develop *sola fide* as an essential part of his theology. In fact, in his landmark translation of the Bible into German, he famously added the word *allein* ("alone") to Romans 3:28: "So halten wir nun dafür, daß der Mensch gerecht werde ohne des Gesetzes Werke, *allein* durch den Glauben"[16] (through faith *alone*).

Due to the efforts of Luther and his contemporaries, *sola fide* has become a cornerstone of Protestant thought. Many believe that any attempt to add human works to the justification equation represents a lack of faith and gives evidence that one is not actually saved; on this basis, many Protestants accuse Catholics of failing to attain salvation based on their differing construal of justification.[17]

For Protestants, the doctrine of *sola fide* has become essentially untouchable. Someone who does not believe in *sola fide* is widely considered to be unsaved and will be targeted for evangelization, even if they are a believer in another faith tradition (i.e., Catholicism or Orthodoxy, the two largest expressions of Christianity in the world). A fellow Protestant who questions the doctrine of *sola fide* is prodding the very heart of Protestantism and is not likely to be treated kindly. Such a person is almost by definition excluded from the intra-faith conversation and Protestantism in general and dismissed as a heretic.

It should come as no surprise that Paul Rainbow's monograph *The Way of Salvation* has received so little attention in Protestant circles. Rainbow points out an alarming flaw with the doctrine of *sola fide*:

> Paul, whose teaching the phrase allegedly epitomizes, never writes it (though he can make frequent use of either "faith" or "alone" independently). The sole occurrence of the phrase "by faith alone" (ἐκ πίστεως μόνον) in the New Testament is in James; and he pointedly rules it out as a way to be justified (James 2:24).[18]

Rainbow's observation can be reduced to two significant points:

1. *Sola fide* appears only once in the New Testament (and never in Paul).

2. It is mentioned only to emphasize that it is utterly rejected as a means of salvation.

The full passage from James reads as follows:

> Do you want to be shown, you foolish person, that faith apart from works is useless? Was not Abraham our father justified by works when he offered up his son Isaac on the altar? You see that faith was active along with his works, and faith was completed by his works; and the Scripture was fulfilled that says, "Abraham believed God, and it was counted to him as righteousness"—and he was called a friend of God. You see that a person is justified by works and *not by faith alone*. (James 2:20–24, emphasis added)

F.C. Baur, a pillar of the famous and influential "Tübingen School" of theology—a liberal Protestant viewpoint—recognized the fundamental incompatibility of James' letter with the traditional interpretation of Paul. He wrote in 1845,

> The main doctrinal position of the Epistle of James: ἐξ ἔργων δικαιοῦται ἄνθρωπος καὶ οὐκ ἐκ πίστεως μόνον, ii. 24, is the direct opposite of the Pauline doctrine as it is stated, Rom. iii. 28, in the proposition, δικαιοῦσθαι πίστει ἄνθρωπον χωρὶς ἔργων νόμου. It cannot be denied that between these two doctrines there exists an essential difference, a direct contradiction.[19]

Here Baur contrasted James 2:24, quoted above, with Romans 3:28, noting that while Paul rules out justification by works in favor of justification by faith, James seems to teach that works are a prerequisite (along with faith) for justification.

Baur was, of course, not the first to discern the apparent contradiction between James and Paul on this point. Luther himself was content to call the Epistle of James an "epistle of straw"; Rainbow remarked that Protestants had rejected Luther's opinion of James without realizing that his doctrine of *sola fide* apparently rested on excising James from the canon. Luther's opinion of James underlies and reinforces his solifidianism.[20]

John Calvin, another father of the Protestant church, held as Luther did to the doctrine of *sola fide*; but instead of deprecating James, he instead tried to harmonize James and Paul:

> We must understand the state of the question, for the dispute here is not respecting the cause of justification, but only what avails a profession of faith without works, and what opinion we are to form of it. Absurdly then do they act who strive to prove by this passage that man is justified by works, because James meant no such thing ... James has quite another thing in view, even to shew that he who professes that he has faith, must prove the reality of his faith by his works. Doubtless James did not mean to teach us here the ground on which our hope of salvation ought to rest; and it is this alone that Paul dwells upon.[21]

Baur dismissed Calvin's insistence on a double meaning for the word "justification"—Paul is speaking of justification before God and James of justification before men. Likewise, he dismissed other harmonization attempts based on redefinitions of the words "faith" and "works"; for Baur, the semantic similarities between the two passages were too great to see them as talking about fundamentally different things.[22] Rather, based on the Pseudo-Clementine Writings, Baur postulated that James and Paul were fundamentally opposed and that Jacobean/Petrine (Jewish) Christianity considered Paul to be a heretic. He further argued that the books of the New Testament that appear to harmonize these two positions, such as the book of Acts, were written much later in an effort to unify the divided church.[23]

While Baur's historical reconstruction of the early church did not stand the test of time due to archeological discoveries that ruined his chronology of the New Testament writings, his basic view that there were two opposing factions in the early church—Hellenists (such as Stephen and Paul) who were against the Temple and the Mosaic Law and Hebrews (such as Peter and James) who remained faithful to the Temple and the Law—persists today.[24]

It is striking to see how influential this paradigm has been even within evangelical Christianity. In a conversation I had over lunch with a local pastor, I mentioned that one of the underlying assumptions of a book I was reading at the time was that the apostles continued to remain faithful to the Temple and the Torah. He agreed but suggested that in this *the apostles were mistaken.*

Here we see Baur's lasting influence. The average Christian may believe that all the apostles were on the same page (i.e., that they rejected the Torah as such). Many learned evangelicals believe (on the basis of the scriptural account and the best modern scholarship) that the Jerusalem church, including the apostles, continued to observe the Torah and worship at the Temple[25] and (on the basis of their theology) that this was *fundamentally incorrect*. As a result, Paul had to come along and correct their understanding, asserting that the Torah and Temple were relics of an earlier era (Judaism) and that God was doing a new thing (Christianity).

> *Many evangelical Christians would rather believe that the apostles were completely and utterly mistaken about the way the Christian life should look than believe that the Torah continues to have an authoritative role in the life of the believer.*

It is telling that the textual evidence for a Torah-observant Jewish church in Jerusalem, headed up by Jewish apostles who continued to observe the Torah, is so strong that evangelicals who do not recognize the continuing authority of the Torah but have taken their study of the Scripture to a higher level have had no choice but to find a way to work around this "problem" of the Jewish Jerusalem church.

As a result, the apostles have become unfortunate casualties. Their authority to teach and act on this subject is tacitly rejected. Many evangelical Christians would rather believe that the apostles were completely and utterly mistaken about the way the Christian life should look than believe that the Torah continues to have an authoritative role in the life of the believer.[26]

Most conservative commentators, however, have historically attempted to harmonize, as Calvin did, James and Paul, rather than set the apostles against one another. James and the Twelve, regardless of their positions of leadership, are absolved from any causal connection to the "Judaizing" tendency of the Jerusalem church; modern scholarship to the contrary, from Baur to Bauckham, is simply rejected.

This is to swerve away from the pit on one side only to fall into the ditch on the other. For as flawed as Baur's paradigm was, and as strong and numerous are the arguments against a strict Hellenist/Hebrew dichotomy in the early church, still there is a reality, impossible to ignore, that the Jerusalem church, or at least a significant element of the Jerusalem church, was unflinchingly Jewish in thought and practice—the text is unambiguous on this point. If Paul was not opposed to the Jerusalem church, and he did not have an ambivalent relationship with the Jerusalem church, then we must remain open to the distinct possibility that he was allied with it (as the Lukan account proposes), and so remains unexplained the contradiction between Paul's concept of justification by faith without works and James' concept of justification by faith along with works.

Throughout all this, scholars have continued to largely agree that the Apostle Paul fought against the Torah or at least against the ceremonial laws. Even if the Jerusalem church did not, Paul fought for *sola fide*—justification by faith alone. Even this core element of Protestant thought has come under increasing attack in the past century.

It has been widely held within Protestantism that Paul's doctrine of *sola fide* was directed specifically against the idea, supposedly part and parcel of Second Temple Judaism, that one was saved through works—and specifically the works of the Mosaic Law, the works of Torah. That the Judaism of Paul's day believed in salvation by works was unequivocally held to be the case by nearly every Protestant commentator and theologian until the twentieth century. Without this backdrop, it makes less sense why Paul would so frequently argue for salvation by faith over and against "works of the law."

Sanders' conclusion was that Jews believed they were "saved" by a gracious act of God in establishing a covenant with their forefather Abraham.

Even scholars who removed justification by faith from the center of Paul's theology (for example, William Wrede and Albert Schweitzer) continued to maintain that justification by faith was to be set against justification by works, though it has been duly noted that in the process of investigating the role of this doctrine in Pauline thought, Wrede and Schweitzer often anticipated later developments.[27]

However, beginning for the most part in the twentieth century, scholars began to question whether Judaism of the first century could really be characterized by dry, lifeless works-righteousness. Scholars such as Claude Montefiore, George Foot Moore, W.D. Davies, and David Daube spent their careers investigating the relationship between Pauline thought and Rabbinic Judaism.

Their work did not garner the attention it deserved in their time, but their influence has been felt deeply through E.P. Sanders' *Paul and Palestinian Judaism*.[28] This work was written in the right style, at the right time, and in the right place to effect a major shift in Pauline studies. Drawing on those scholars who preceded him in comparing Paul and Rabbinic Judaism, Sanders painstakingly investigated large swaths of Jewish literature to build a coherent picture of what could be termed Jewish soteriology in the Second Temple Period. His conclusion was that Jews believed they were "saved" by a gracious act of God in establishing a covenant with their forefather Abraham. The role of works in this process was merely to retain one's identity as a covenant member. Sanders termed this paradigm "covenantal nomism."

All at once, without the foil of works-righteousness Judaism with which to compare Paul, the traditional interpretation of Paul ceased to make sense. This was keenly demonstrated a few years after the publication of *Paul and Palestinian Judaism* by James D.G. Dunn, who argued that if Second Temple Judaism was not based on works-righteousness, then a Paul who argued against works-righteousness was incomprehensible.[29]

Dunn went on to argue that "works of the law" in Paul did not refer to the commandments of the Torah as a whole. Rather, it referred to those commandments that were specific markers of Jewish identity such as dietary laws, Sabbath observance, and circumcision. Dunn's Paul sought to invalidate these commandments to unite Jew and Gentile in one body so that Gentile converts could be justified not by "works of the law"—that is, by becoming Jewish—but by faith in Jesus Christ alone. So Paul argued not against works-righteousness but against the presumption of salvation on the basis of being Jewish.[30] Dunn's essay spawned an entirely new approach to Paul that is now called the New Perspective on Paul.

Recognizing that Dunn's Paul is still substantially anti-Jewish in that he invalidates Jewish religious and ethnic identity within the church, many scholars have begun to postulate that Paul retained a positive relationship with Judaism and even a continuing self-identity within Judaism. This approach, often termed the "Radical New Perspective" or "Beyond the New

Perspective," holds that Paul argued against the "works of the law" only for Gentile converts; Jewish believers were still to obey all the commandments, including those that were markers of Jewish identity. Consequently, Jewish and Gentile believers in the church were expected to coexist as one body while maintaining their respective social identities.[31]

Rather, the faithfulness of Jesus Christ to complete the mission that God assigned him resulted in the justification of God's people.

In this paradigm, justification by faith is thought to be a doctrine developed by Paul solely to explain how Gentile believers are saved. It is not some foundational theological concept that explains how humanity as a whole is reconciled to God. Rather, it is Paul's justification of his Gentile mission.

The phrase "justification by faith" has come under attack from yet another angle. A little before the turn of the century, scholars began to wonder whether justification by "faith in Jesus Christ" (Romans 3:22; Galatians 2:16) was the best translation of the Greek phrase πίστεως Ἰησοῦ Χριστοῦ. Many scholars now believe that this translation, while one of several technically accurate possibilities, does not capture Paul's intention. Rather, they put forward an alternate translation, which is also technically correct: "through the faithfulness of Jesus Christ."[32]

If this latter translation is correct, then Paul was not arguing that people are saved by placing their faith in Jesus. Rather, the faithfulness of Jesus Christ to complete the mission that God assigned him resulted in the justification of God's people.

Another line of attack that has been brought to bear on *sola fide* is the idea, now taken for granted by historical-critical studies on Paul's letters, that Paul did not intend to write theological dissertations. Rather, he was addressing specific problems in the churches to which he wrote. Even the epistle to the Romans was not written to outline Paul's theology of salvation, as classical Protestant thinkers have often thought. Rather, he seeks to address some problem in the church at Rome or to accomplish something related to his mission to Gaul. Scholars often disagree on what Paul's specific aims were, but there is a broad consensus that Paul's epistles were situational and not intended to be used to develop a systematic theology.

These developments, taken together, have caused some to ring the death knell for *sola fide*. Now seen as Martin Luther's backlash against what he saw as an overly legalistic Roman Catholic Church, its exegetical basis has been severely challenged.

The Protestant response has varied. A conservative introduction to the New Testament—for example, D.A. Carson and Douglas Moo's contribution—may dismiss the most prolific scholar of the Radical New Perspective on Paul with two sentences;[33] it often appears that traditional scholars simply do not find arguments from this perspective to be worth engaging.

It is more common for traditional scholars to engage the historical scholarship that has formed the basis for modern views of Paul. So in an effort to cast doubt on Sanders' conception of Second Temple Judaism, which has enjoyed support from a broad consensus of scholars for decades, conservative scholars published a two-volume response with contributions from a wide range of scholars.[34]

A more constructive approach has been advocated by Michael Bird, who has endeavored to find areas of confluence between the old and new perspectives on Paul. He finds several areas of broad correlation, areas that can be counted as common ground from which to further the discussion. He advocates this approach rather than, as Carson and others have attempted, having scholars try to dismantle one another's core positions.[35]

Yet the hostility that many conservative scholars have displayed toward Sanders and Dunn and their tendency to dismiss the Radical New Perspective (a category that neatly describes the views of many Messianic Jewish scholars) betray an understanding that traditional views of Paul and the New Testament—and particularly of justification by faith—are threatened by the last few centuries of historical-critical scholarship. This threat has intensified with the proliferation of monographs advocating a Jewish Paul who continued to recognize the Jewish people as God's chosen people and the Torah's continuing binding authority for God's people.

Chapter Four

SOLA FIDE   PART 2

The words *sola fide*, "by faith alone," describe an event called justification—the term used in Protestant theology to describe the declaration by God that a sinner is now righteous. Since, according to Christian theology, only the righteous and not sinners will be given eternal life, this declaration of righteousness by God, or justification, lies at the heart of soteriology, the study of salvation.

Sola fide therefore, along with *sola scriptura*, stands at the very heart of Protestantism. Ask a Reformed Protestant what the gospel message is, and some version of "justification by faith alone" is likely to be the answer. It is a central, pivotal piece of the theological puzzle.

In the previous chapter, I explored how the scriptural foundations for the doctrine of justification by faith alone have been apparently undermined by the last few centuries of critical scholarship, up to and including the New Perspective on Paul. Many scholars no longer believe that Paul intended to teach that people are saved simply by an act of belief when he used the terminology "justified by faith."

The dichotomy between these scholars and their traditional counterparts (those who continue to embrace justification by faith as the central and defining aspect of salvation) is not a matter of mere intellectual disagreement. It is a fervent debate with hard feelings and harsh words on both sides. It has been borne out in popular literature as the ongoing debate between N.T. Wright, who espouses a view of justification informed by the New Perspective on Paul, and John Piper, a staunch advocate of the traditional view.

The sheer volume of literature on the subject and the intensity of the continuing debate both testify to the fact that the issue is far from settled. One cannot imagine, at this point, traditional scholars backpedaling from their firm denouncements of the New Perspective on Paul. Neither is the New Perspective and its many offshoots in any danger of losing their relevance in a post-Holocaust world.

While many Messianic Jewish scholars have embraced something like the Radical New Perspective approach to Paul,[36] a domain of scholarship whose path was blazed by the New Perspective, Messianic Judaism has also traditionally striven to cultivate a positive relationship with evangelical Christianity, the movement out of which it was born.

As a result, there exists a sort of tension in Messianic Jewish theology between the need to affirm and be affirmed by the broader Yeshua movement (that is, Christianity) and the need to embrace a theology of justification and salvation that is built on a Jewish understanding of Paul's epistles. It will not do to burn bridges with the institutional church, but neither will it do to compromise the essentially Jewish character of the movement.

While it is one thing for organized Messianic Judaism to adopt a clearly different theology of justification from that of the non-Jewish wing of the church, it is quite another for a non-Jewish believer like myself to adopt a Jewish theology of justification. Messianic Judaism can provide a home for those

Jewish believers who are at the forefront of developing Messianic Jewish theology; I, on the other hand, have no spiritual home but the church. Therefore, it is even more imperative that my own theology of justification be sufficiently congruent with that of the church, and yet I feel the same need a Jewish believer might feel to embrace an authentically Jewish theology of justification—making my position, in my opinion, decidedly more difficult.

I use myself as an example because I suspect that many readers will find themselves in a position similar to mine—not willing to divorce the church but also unwilling to compromise on what we see as a fundamentally needed change in Christian theology. Caught in the crossfire between critical scholars and conservative stalwarts, we must carefully navigate this middle ground.

Broader Horizons

Not wishing to rush in where angels fear to tread, which in this case is an area of scholarship that is hotly contested by highly educated and motivated scholars, we will not seek to establish a complete theology of justification in this chapter. However, we must at least address the pressing issue of the role of works in salvation. What does this look like from a Jewish perspective? To begin to answer this, we need to zoom out a little bit and discuss the underlying terms and factors at work here.

The core idea here is that of the causal factor. There is no question of whether works are a necessary part of the life of a believer. Both Protestants and Catholics believe that works are necessary, non-negotiable, not optional. The difference is that in Roman Catholic theology, works are a causal factor—in other words, they contribute toward justification. In Protestant theology, works are not a causal factor—they contribute nothing toward justification; rather, they are only evidence of justification.

Justification, in turn, is the basis on which the believer is saved. When we are justified, we are no longer reckoned as sinners but as righteous. However, is this declaration of righteousness forensic—in other words, is this declaration made without any basis of righteous behavior on the part of the one who is justified?—or is it an accurate statement to the effect that the believer is now truly righteous and behaves righteously?

This question is an important one. Traditional Protestant theology sees justification as purely forensic; the righteousness of Christ is reckoned to the believer's account, so to speak, without any actual righteousness produced or evidenced on the part of the believer. Luther's famous distillation of this principle is the Latin phrase *simul justus et peccator*, meaning at once (forensically) righteous while (in actuality) a sinner. In Protestant theology the process by which the believer actually becomes righteous is instead called "sanctification," and this is seen as a totally separate action on God's part (though as parts of the salvation process, justification and sanctification are related).

However, if Paul intended to say, as Roman Catholic theologians often argue, that justification describes a process by which the believer *becomes righteous* in point of fact, then Paul's language of justification takes on an entirely different meaning.

Making use of Paul Rainbow's monograph, *The Way of Salvation*, we can see that some scholars posit that both views are true. When the believer first decides to follow Christ, he is justified "in advance." This justification is forensic; it can be called a legal fiction in that the believer is not actually fully righteous in thought and deed. However, it anticipates a reality that is coming. Later, upon one's death and final judgment, the believer is justified a second time. This time, however, the declaration of righteousness reflects the actual state of the believer—once and for all, finally and truly righteous.

While this increasingly complicated *ordo salutis*, or order of salvation, does seem to make better sense of Paul's writings in that Paul does appear at times to use one or the other sense of justification, it begins to provoke the question: Why would two different justifications be needed? Surely God, who sees the end from the beginning, requires only one declaration of righteousness to properly classify the believer.

At this point, we begin to understand why one of the great formative doctrinal frameworks of traditional Protestantism—Calvinism, and specifically predestination—came to the forefront very quickly alongside the Five *Solae*. Of course, only one declaration of righteousness is needed, and this declaration, in Calvinist theology, ultimately comes apart from any volitional act on the part of the believer. In other words, neither faith nor works are ultimately *the* causal factors; rather, the believer is justified because he is elected, because he is predestined to be saved. He demonstrates faith because he is chosen—he is not chosen on the basis of his faith. While justification may technically be declared on the basis of the believer's faith, this entire process is essentially out of his control; even his own faith does not come of his own volition. Seen this way, it is hardly appropriate to say that the believer's faith truly influences God's actions in relation to justification in any meaningful way.

In taking this stream of thought to its logical conclusion, we would depart completely from any remotely Jewish understanding of the Scripture. Judaism takes for granted the choice of the individual person. The Jewish conception of God is indeed reactive in the sense that God's actions toward his people depend on their actions and responses to him. While it may seem illogical that the God who sees the end from the beginning would act specifically in response to some human action or belief, this human-divine relationship, in which there are give and take and push and pull on the part of both God and man, lies at the foundation of Jewish thought and philosophy. To see Abraham, the "first Jew," negotiate with God for the souls of Sodom and Gomorrah is typical of this foundational belief that God does indeed respond to us and even that we can, if such a thing is possible, determine what God's actions will be in a given situation.

The Jewish conception of God is indeed reactive in the sense that God's actions toward his people depend on their actions and responses to him.

Is it possible for us to zoom out even more? Can we reconcile the Augustinian/Calvinist mode of thinking about God, in which God's infinite knowledge and power preclude any real choice on the part of the human being, with the Jewish mode of thinking about God, in which the relationship between God and man is dynamic and vital? After all, either destination can be reached from Scripture; the God a person ends up seeing will depend upon the logical pathways the reader chooses to follow—and, as we will see, upon the reader's conception of time and space and God's relationship to these constructs.

Time and Space

The *ordo salutis* is a sequence of events. A simplified Protestant *ordo salutis* may be something like this: predestination, calling, regeneration, faith, justification, sanctification, glorification. These steps happen in this order. One's faith precedes his justification, but predestination precedes faith, and so forth. Other steps may be added; in Rainbow's scheme, another justification is added toward the end. Arminians would be loath to accept this *ordo salutis* without adding foreknowledge before predestination (so that God's decision to predestine the believer is dependent on the believer's decision of faith, to which God reacts "in advance" through his foreknowledge).

But what if the *ordo salutis* is a fundamentally flawed mental construct?

What if it causes us to see causal factors that are actually absent? Or to miss causal factors that are in reality present?

A truly Jewish conception of God does include push and pull, give and take. Ultimately, a truly Jewish conception of God also includes the idea of the *ein sof*, the ineffable, the inaccessible domain of God's real person, which is completely beyond human understanding in every possible way. Even in rational Judaism, epitomized by the Rambam, it is affirmed that God is so exalted that whatever we may conceive of him in our limited minds will ultimately be deficient.

Consider that God is infinite. He is completely unbounded. This unboundedness must naturally include time. Time is a construct; Albert Einstein taught us that it is only one dimension in the larger fabric of space-time. It is not an absolute reality; rather, it is created and sustained by God and is external to his very being. God is not subservient to time; rather, he transcends time.

How does an *ordo salutis* fit into the concept of a God who does not experience time—or at least, does not have to experience it?

This is a question that was far more difficult to answer, or even ask, before the scientific revolution brought on by Einstein and his world-changing theories on the nature of time. It would have been impossible for the venerable saints who articulated traditional Protestant theology to imagine the universe as Einstein did. Their theology went hand in hand with their philosophy and their metaphysics. Today's theologians must reckon with a new physics, one that had never before been conceived—relativistic physics, in which time and space, matter and energy, are linked in unforeseen ways.

Consider the difference between God's experience of time and ours. To the human viewer, who is trapped inside what appears to be a sequential series of events, one thing may happen and then another. But is this the way God, who created time, experiences time? Does God, who is above, beyond, and outside all created existence, see things one after another? Or all at once?

Imagine a fantastically precise 3-D printing machine that lays down one layer of molecules at a time. Imagine then that a program is given to the machine. It begins to print, and layer by layer, sheet by sheet, molecules are printed on top of each other, each layer differing slightly from the last. Over time, these layers begin to form a shape. After the machine is done with its work, a statuette of Saint Paul has been printed.

Now imagine being able to see only one layer at a time. It would be extraordinarily difficult to tell what was being formed.

Physics in a post-Einstein world teaches us that time is similar to this. Time is one dimension of space-time. Every Planck unit of time that goes by is like one layer being laid on top of the previous one. We see each unit of time sequentially. An outside observer, however, would be able to see all units of time at once. Therefore, instead of a trillion sheets of molecules, we see a plastic Saint Paul; instead of a trillion moments in time, God sees all reality, all time, at once.

God does not need to see that decision "before" it happens and make decisions "before" their causal factors; with God, ultimately, there is no before and after.

In the end, does the sequence of molecule layers printed by our 3-D printing machine matter? Does it matter that Saint Paul's feet were printed before his head? No. When we see the final product, no single layer has any significance drawn from the order in which it was laid down. We see simply Saint Paul in miniature.

When God looks at us, does he not then see our predestination, our faith, our justification, our glorification—in no particular order? In God's eyes, is our end not already seen alongside our beginning? Can there be said to be a beginning and an end in the sense that we understand them?

Can we see both Calvinism and Judaism represented here? Clearly, our "predestination" is obvious, if God sees all time "at once." On the other side of the coin, we do not need to postulate that God's foreknowledge has a determinative effect on our actions; rather, because God sees all at once, God's foreknowledge is simply a function of his existence outside of time. Therefore, we have a concept of predestination and foreknowledge that does not eliminate causal factors such as the believer's decision to follow Jesus. God does not need to see that decision "before" it happens and make decisions "before" their causal factors; with God, ultimately, there is no before and after.

It is possible to see that no matter how deterministic one's outlook, God's actions toward us can still be based on the shape we cause our lives to take. After all, what our tomorrow looks like will depend on the decisions we make today. The very shape of the future comes in part from the actions of human beings. In the totality of God's perception, all the decisions we make are "simultaneous" with the very fact of our existence. To exist is to be fully known by God.

On what basis does God justify the believer? By the person's decision to follow Jesus? Or by a life lived in devotion to Jesus? Is justification forensic? Or a declaration that the believer is in fact truly righteous?

The answer is that God's decision to justify the believer is based on the total package. All is seen by him at once, from the beginning to the end: the decision to follow Jesus, the life of discipleship, believing Jesus' message, faithful adherence to Jesus' teachings. Ultimately, I do not believe that these concepts need to be (or even can be) teased out or separated into categories.

The ramifications of this assertion are easiest to see in the case of a former believer who has abandoned faith. In answer to the question, "Did that person lose his salvation?" a Calvinist would answer, "No; he was never saved to begin with because God did not elect him." An Arminian would answer, "Yes, he lost his salvation."

But here we would answer, "God's decision to save or not save will be based on the entire picture of a person's life, past, present, and future all tied together inextricably into one coherent and eternally consistent package. One cannot become saved and then lose his salvation; on the other hand, no one is saved until the final judgment is pronounced, the entire picture is seen, and death is finally conquered; and on the third hand, for a saved person to exist is for that person to be saved; and on the fourth hand, the person is saved because of his volitional response to God's initiative of grace."

Salvation Science

If we can be permitted to zoom out one more time and perhaps to put a wide-angle lens on the whole topic of soteriology, let us pose this question: Why is it important to know who is saved and who is not?

The functional expression of soteriology is to help us draw lines between those who have been saved and those who have not been. As believers, we want that line to be clear so that we will know when someone has crossed over it—so that we will know whether *we* have crossed over it. We want to be sure that we are saved, and we want to be sure of who else is saved.

Why do we want this?

That may seem like a stupid question. But I think that if we were to answer it truthfully, most of us would say that we want to be sure that we have fulfilled whatever qualifications God has put in place for us to procure eternal life. After all, there is no greater reward or gift than glorification and immortality. This has always been the case; the four-thousand-year-old *Epic of Gilgamesh* reflects an aspect of humanity that has always longed to conquer death. So if the Bible was written to show us how to become immortal, then we want to be sure that we understand it correctly and that we follow whatever directions it gives us toward that end.

Most of the Bible is about God's relationship with the Jewish people, a topic that has no place in traditional Christian soteriology.

With that answer, it is instructive to go back and read the Gospels of Matthew, Mark, and Luke. Does it seem as if Jesus came to teach man how to become immortal? Is that the point of the Bible or even of the New Testament or even of the Gospels? Is that the purpose of Jesus' teaching ministry?

When we collapse the gospel narrative into systematic theology, we run the terrible risk of losing the forest for the trees. When we base our soteriology on the Gospel of John and the Epistle to the Romans and then read the rest of the Bible through that soteriological lens, we largely miss the point, because most of the Bible is not about how to become immortal.

Most of the Bible is about God's relationship with the Jewish people, a topic that has no place in traditional Christian soteriology.

At the risk of oversimplifying, I will invoke a basic principle that has guided my study of the Bible for many years: If we have put ourselves in a position in which we have to choose between the Bible and our theology, let's set aside our theology and re-examine the Bible.

In that spirit, let us engage a seminal lecture by Messianic Jewish theologian Mark Kinzer entitled "Final Destinies:

Qualifications for Receiving an Eschatological Inheritance."[37] Kinzer makes the point that when we examine the topic of final destinies, or "salvation," in the Christian sense of the word, we tend to read the Synoptic Gospels through the lens of the theology of John and Paul.

If we were instead to take the Synoptic Gospels first—they are, after all, given pride of place in the canon, and we know that the Petrine tradition on which they are based took shape earlier than the others—then we are surprised to find that, as Kinzer puts it, "one of the primary themes in this tradition's approach to final destinies is the warning against presumption: the misplaced confidence that we will be rewarded at the end, while others (who do not possess our qualifications) will be punished."[38]

Does this sound familiar?

A Protestant who believes in *sola fide* will find confidence in his salvation because he has placed his faith in Jesus. But Matthew wrote,

> Not everyone who says to me, "Lord, Lord," will enter the kingdom of heaven, but only the one who does the will of my Father in heaven. On that day many will say to me, "Lord, Lord, did we not prophesy in your name, and cast out demons in your name, and do many deeds of power in your name?" Then I will declare to them, "I never knew you; go away from me, you evildoers." (Matthew 7:21–23 NRSV)

Kinzer elaborates on this passage:

> This is an extremely significant text. It is not addressed to casual hearers of Yeshua, but to those who speak and act publicly in his name—and do so

effectively! It is addressed to leaders of the Yeshua-movement—to us! Like the "heirs of the kingdom" in general, we must guard against the presumption that our participation and fruitful leadership in the community of the (renewed) covenant ensures our final destiny.[39]

If we are relying on a soteriology that declares the delineation between lost and saved at the boundary line of *sola fide* to inform our opinion on who is going to live forever and who is going to be condemned, then we are choosing to ignore large swaths of the apostolic tradition—the New Testament—at our peril.

This is why I do not believe it is fruitful to engage in the minutia of debate surrounding solifidianism and its role in forming a theology of salvation or a theology of Paul or a theology of Jesus until the question is asked: Are *sola fide* and Christian soteriology in general useful as tools to help us delineate between saved and unsaved, or have we already missed the point of Jesus' message by asking the questions that soteriology seeks to answer?

The Easy Way

One can find passage after passage in the New Testament about inheriting the kingdom of heaven, about inheriting eternal life. But Protestant theology chooses to hyperfocus on a few of these passages to the detriment of all the rest.

The "Romans Road" of Scripture passages is a stellar example of this principle in action. Chosen because of their congruence with *sola fide*, the Romans Road is a collection of verses scattered throughout the Epistle to the Romans that, placed together, appear to teach that the golden ticket to immortality is to believe that Jesus is God and that he rose from the dead. But surely, if Paul's intention was to teach this, he would have placed those verses together for us, rather than sending us on a scavenger hunt through his epistle. One could just as easily cherry pick a different passage from Romans to teach a very different road to salvation:

> He will render to each one according to his works: to those who by patience in well-doing seek for glory and honor and immortality, he will give eternal life; but for those who are self-seeking and do not obey the truth, but obey unrighteousness, there will be wrath and fury. There will be tribulation and distress for every human being who does evil, the Jew first and also the Greek, but glory and honor and peace for everyone who does good, the Jew first and also the Greek. (Romans 2:6–10)

There it is—works-based salvation, in the heart of Paul's *magnum opus*. And this passage has the advantage over the Romans Road in that it is found all in one paragraph.

Just as this passage has its proper place in Paul's larger argument, so do the verses of the Romans Road. To pull either set of verses out in isolation is to use the Bible in ways it was never intended to be used.

So why have we chosen the Romans Road over Romans 2:6–10 as the quintessential set of verses on salvation? Perhaps because salvation by faith alone, *sola fide*, is the path of least resistance to salvation. It is the "cheapest" immortality to be found anywhere. In its most simplified and reductionist form, *sola fide* teaches that nothing is required on the part of the believer except the adoption of a certain Christology.

Of course, Reformed theologians do not really believe that nothing else is required of the believer. A good Reformed theologian would consider this position to be an abuse of *sola fide*. Reformed theology is quite robust on the subject of doing good works. To join a Reformed church is by no means the path of least resistance; Reformed believers are rigorous in doing good works. However, these works, in Reformed theology, do not effect the salvation of the believer. They are necessary in the life of a disciple of Christ, but they contribute nothing toward the believer's status before God.

As Kinzer's lecture demonstrates, however, there is far more to the kingdom of heaven, to eternal life, to our status before God, than *sola fide*, or purely forensic righteousness. Whether we examine the Synoptics, the general epistles, or the Pauline epistles, we find in every case that the bar is actually very high for one who wishes to enter the kingdom of heaven. We find in Matthew 7, quoted above, that Jesus taught his disciples not to assume that their status as believers automatically granted them eternal life; rather, they were told to focus on their works and to make sure that they were living up to the standards of the kingdom of heaven.

As we discussed above, to tease out justification, sanctification, glorification, predestination, and other aspects of salvation into separate and distinct categories is to set ourselves up to fundamentally misunderstand the salvation process. More importantly for this discussion, for us to remove the works of the kingdom of heaven from the salvific equation is to reduce salvation to something less than it is portrayed to be in the New Testament—that is, when the whole is considered and not only a few verses in isolation.

Paul and Jesus

Having laid this foundation, when we begin to reappraise the many arguments surrounding justification in Paul's epistles, we find that we have a few more tools with which to evaluate how Paul may have viewed the operation of salvation in the life of a believer.

I assume here that Paul agreed with Jesus' teachings. This viewpoint, however, is not possible to take for granted in serious academic study of Paul, and, in fact, it is common in academia to see Paul as abandoning much of what Jesus taught in favor of a novel theology of salvation. But as a believer writing to other believers, I do not feel the need to belabor this point except to say that if Paul did not agree with Jesus, there would be no reason for a believer to adopt Paul's opinion to begin with.

If Paul embraced Jesus' more complex and multifaceted view of salvation as expressed in the Synoptic tradition, then what can we make of Paul's assertion that believers are saved solely by faith in Jesus Christ? Or perhaps Richard Hays is right to translate the phrase "faith in Jesus Christ" (Galatians 3:22) as "the faithfulness of Jesus Christ"?[40]

Sigve Tonstad's monograph on this Greek phrase *pistis Iesou* asserts that it "will tolerate [for its interpretation] any one of four main alternatives, 'the faithfulness of Jesus,' 'the faith of Jesus,' 'faith in Jesus,' or 'faithfulness to Jesus.'"[41] He further notes, though his exploration of the phrase is confined to the Apocalypse of John, that if his larger argument is correct, "the larger picture then emerging will tend to defuse the constricting effect of picking one wording before another."[42] I have chosen to use Tonstad's wording here, but many scholars who embrace Hays' analysis of *pistis Iesou* would agree with Tonstad's basic interpretive premise—that is, our "larger picture" of Paul's theology will often dictate which reading and which translation we choose.

To apply this same reasoning to Paul, we can say that if Paul embraced Jesus' teaching on the qualifications for eternal life, then in Paul's writings the phrase *pistis Iesou* would be translated in such a way as to harmonize Paul's teachings with what Jesus had already taught. The "larger picture" will dictate our interpretation of Paul.

While we are begging the question, it is nonetheless true that the way *pistis Iesou* is translated and understood by a Reformed theologian will also depend on his perspective on Paul and Paul's soteriology. In every case, when more than one option is available to us, we will generally understand a text as reinforcing our own theological position if it is possible to do so within the bounds of technically correct translation. If we consider the Petrine tradition as part of Paul's broader interpretive context, then it is no great leap of logic to interpret Paul through the lens of that tradition.

If Hays and the scholars who follow him are correct, a verse like Galatians 3:22, translated in the English Standard Version as "But the Scripture imprisoned everything under sin, so that the promise by faith in Jesus Christ [*pisteos Iesou Christou*] might be given to those who believe [*pisteuousin*]," could instead carry the meaning "... so that the promise [i.e., eternal life] born out of the faithfulness of Jesus Christ [i.e., his completed mission] might be given to those who are faithful"—in other words, to those who "bear good fruit" (Matthew 7:15-20), to those who are not "workers of lawlessness" (Matthew 7:21-23), to the one who "hears these words of [Jesus] and does them" (Matthew 7:24-27).

In other words, to reject the forensic righteousness of Luther and Calvin in favor of the New Perspective on Paul is to begin the process of unwinding Protestant theology as a whole.

And if James Dunn is correct in asserting that "works of the law" refers to specific practices that demark the Jewish community from the surrounding nations,[43] then Galatians 2:16, translated as "Yet we know that a person is not justified by works of the law but through faith in Jesus Christ, so we also have believed in Christ Jesus, in order to be justified by faith in Christ and not by works of the law, because by works of the law no one will be justified," might instead carry the meaning, "Yet we know that a person does not become righteous by becoming Jewish but through faithfulness to Jesus Christ [i.e., through cleaving to him and following his teachings], so we also have been faithful to Christ Jesus, in order to be made righteous through faithfulness to Christ and not by being Jewish, because by becoming Jewish no one will be made righteous."

It seems that if we are to expect Paul to follow Jesus in his theology of salvation, then we must prefer the New Perspective to the traditional view of Paul. The arguments of Dunn, Hays, and others have the potential to bring Paul in line with the earlier apostolic tradition—that is, the Synoptic Gospels—in this matter.

A traditional objection to the New Perspective, however, has been its seeming inability to deal with theological questions. What of an *ordo salutis*? What of the science of salvation?

To use a traditional theologian's own words: "The Reformers ... strenuously maintained the forensic thesis, not simply because of confessional polemics: the *theological* stakes are too high for any compromise to be accepted."[44]

In other words, to reject the forensic righteousness of Luther and Calvin in favor of the New Perspective on Paul is to begin the process of unwinding Protestant theology as a whole. It is to say, as the Reformers did, that the church and her doctors have been wrong. It is to erase thick black lines of demarcation. It is to un-answer many deep and unsettling questions that have been thought answered for hundreds of years. Many pastors and theologians continue to regard this as an unacceptable outcome. But why?

Is it so bad to leave these questions unanswered? In a world in which God's conception of time is the only relevant one regarding the mechanics of our salvation, can we do anything else but resign ourselves to the fact that the full scope of God's action on our behalf is beyond our understanding?

If we truly serve a God whose thoughts and actions take place outside of time, we must remind ourselves of our inability to fully grasp these thoughts and actions and their relationship to ours. It seems rather imprudent to rely on a theological system to smooth the bumps in the text of the New Testament that inevitably arise from the interference of an extra-dimensional, omnipotent, omniscient being—especially when that system causes us to leave such passages as the Sermon on the Mount outside of a conversation on righteousness, justification, and the fate of the dead.

Rather, an awareness of our fundamental lack of ability to comprehend God leaves us free to simply take Jesus and Paul at face value and to live in the immense and disturbing tension between our confidence in the atoning work of Jesus Christ and our own tenuous position as sinners continually in need of repentance.

Conclusion

So where does that leave *sola fide*?

Like *sola scriptura*, *sola fide* was born out of an intense conflict between Protestants and Catholics during the most formative years of the Protestant tradition. It was designed specifically to counter various practices in the Catholic Church that Luther felt were not represented in Scripture.

However, regardless of whether Luther was justified in his reproach of the Catholic Church, to take *sola fide* as a broad interpretive paradigm is to shut off many avenues of biblical discussion about justification, soteriology, and the final destinies of individuals. It is to render the Synoptic tradition virtually unintelligible insofar as it speaks to these issues.

It is not hard to understand why many Messianic Jewish theologians have landed on the Radical New Perspective wing of the Paul debate. Not only does the "Jewish" Paul guard the Torah, the Jewish people, and their traditional way of life, but he also can be harmonized with the teachings of the Master on theological subjects about which, in critical scholarship, the two have often been seen at odds: specifically, the way to attain eternal life.

What implications does this have for the relationship between Messianic Judaism and evangelical Protestantism?

I can't speak for Messianic Judaism, but as a friend to the movement, I would encourage Messianic Jewish scholars to contribute to the New Perspective debate, to "restore an historical voice to the contemporary discussion."[45] That process of dialogue will give Messianic Judaism the opportunity to form a coherent theology of Paul that can be located on a map of broader Christian theology.

The Messianic Jewish Paul will be unique to Messianic Judaism. However, he will not be completely different from the Paul recognized by traditional Protestants. Keeping the lines of dialogue open will allow Messianic ideas to find an audience in the church, and it will keep Messianic Judaism from separating itself completely from Christian thought.

The New Perspective debate has already stretched and tested the ability of fellow believers to remain friends when they find themselves to be theological rivals. Theologically conservative Protestants have often shown themselves unwilling to build bridges between themselves and other Christians who embrace a different theology. This problem has the potential to be compounded when the bridge is being built to a group that does not identify as "Christian" but rather as "Jewish" in its essential character.

So while Messianic Judaism will likely find *sola fide* to be unacceptable as an interpretive paradigm, Messianic Jews will find that engaging traditional Protestants on this issue will require grace, creativity, a willingness to find common ground, and a strong scriptural foundation from which to argue their position.

The starting point for this discussion must be Jesus. If Jesus' followers can be convinced to begin building their theology on Jesus' teachings, if we are willing to incorporate the Synoptic Gospels into our theology as readily as we incorporate John and Paul, then perhaps we can be made to see that we have missed part of the picture and that eternal life and salvation cannot be reduced to a quick formula or a verbal or mental elixir of life.

Chapter Five

SOLA GRATIA

Sola gratia, "by grace alone," is the third of the Five *Solae*, five condensed theological statements that helped define the Protestant Reformation. The previous four chapters examined *sola scriptura* and *sola fide* and showed them to be of questionable usefulness in shaping Messianic Jewish theology. However, due to their foundational importance in Protestant theology, those who are pushing for what they feel is a more authentic first-century Jewish definition of what it means to be a disciple must tread carefully when discussing them.

Sola gratia, however, invites its own set of difficulties.

The essential definition of *sola gratia* is that salvation comes by God's grace alone and not because of any merit on the part of the one saved. It is hard to imagine anyone having a different view—the view that some people do not need God's grace, that some people do not need for God to overlook, cover, or provide atonement for their sins.

In fact, the very inclusion of *sola gratia* in the Five *Solae* raises some pressing questions about the Protestant conception of other faiths.

Those acquainted with the Reformation will know of the role played by indulgences, acts of penitence, the viewing of relics, and other "works" that were thought to shorten one's stay in purgatory. Luther's ninety-five theses, his first shot over the bow of the Catholic Church, were primarily concerned with indulgences, letters from the Pope that lessened one's temporal punishment—that is, purgation—for venial sin. Luther perceived the practice of granting indulgences in his day as a corruption of its original purpose, having been reduced to a financial transaction that guaranteed immediate salvation for those trapped in purgatory and absolution of sins for those still living, a transaction cynically abused by some of the church's *quaestors* to raise funds for lavish building projects.

The idea was formulated in response to specific abuses of the late Medieval Period, abuses that are today condemned by Christians of all denominations, including Catholics.

From this seed grew *sola gratia*: It is by God's grace alone that one is saved. God's grace cannot be purchased by doing good works or viewing relics or giving money to the church—otherwise, it is not grace at all but a transaction in which the believer gains leverage over God. Instead, grace is given on God's initiative and cannot be earned. It may be actualized in response to some action on the part of the believer—that is, contrition and repentance, as Luther so eloquently argued in his theses—but these actions do not give the penitent leverage over God, as it were. Rather, they open the way for God's grace to be communicated to the penitent.[46]

The thing is, *sola gratia* does not conflict with Catholic doctrine. The idea was formulated in response to specific abuses of the late Medieval Period, abuses that are today condemned by Christians of all denominations, including Catholics. The overzealous *quaestors* were out of line with historical Catholic doctrine, and in response to the widespread outcry associated with the Reformation, the practice of selling indulgences was reigned in by the Catholic Church at the Council of Trent.

While Catholics and Protestants still deeply disagree over the nature of justification (as we have explored in previous chapters), the essential belief that the sinner is saved by God's grace alone is shared by all.

Many (most?) Protestants[47] continue to uphold *sola gratia* as a distinctive Protestant doctrine. It is hard not to interpret this stance as an accusation that Roman Catholics do not believe that grace alone provides the basis for salvation.

Therefore, we must raise a larger question here: Who gets to decide what Catholics believe?

This question will lead us into a broader discussion on the relationship between Judaism and Christianity, a discussion that is particularly relevant for Messianic Judaism. Roman Catholics are not the only target of *sola gratia*. While the Protestant Reformation was the impetus for the formation of *sola gratia*, Protestant Christians widely believe that both Catholics *and Jews* rely on some degree of earned merit for salvation and not solely on the grace of God.

To expand our question, then, who gets to decide what Jews believe? Or what anyone else believes?

Definition

It is a poorly understood but accurate statement that people, denominations, and religions tend to define themselves by what makes them *different* from each other rather than by what lies at the *core* of their identity.

Let's say that I have a friend who is honest, trustworthy, intelligent, friendly, has a good sense of humor, takes care of her children, and doesn't like chocolate. When I introduce her as such to others, for which of these traits do you think she will be remembered? Most people see themselves as honest, intelligent, and so on. It is far less common to meet someone who doesn't like chocolate. So, my friend will be known as the one who doesn't like chocolate rather than the honest one or the friendly one.

How close does her aversion to chocolate lie to the core of her being, her self-identity, her essential character? Not close at all. In the end, this culinary disposition is incidental to the question of *who she is*.

This tendency to reduce self-definition to the question of "what makes me unique" rather than "what is really important to me" is universal, and it can be seen in the formative years of the church. The Nicene Creed, for example, was originally formulated at the First Council of Nicaea in 325 CE to distinguish "orthodox" Christianity from the Arian heresy. The creed itself does not give its reader many clues as to the actual substance of the teachings of Jesus Christ. There is no moral or ethical content in it, though such would be expected in a definition of a religion based on the teachings of the rabbi who delivered the Sermon on the Mount.

Rather, the creed centers on the Greek word ὁμοούσιον, *Homoousion*, "of one substance"—the word chosen by the council to describe Jesus' relationship with the Father. Arius and his followers, from what we can tell, did not conceive of Jesus in this way and so were excluded from normative Christianity on the basis of this creed. This, in fact, was the creed's primary purpose.

However, today many Christians believe that this creed is the central or defining component of Christianity. One who believes that Jesus is of one substance with the Father and that he died and was raised again (also mentioned in the Nicene Creed) has attained eternal life.

"Not Arian" is not a good definition of "Christian." Not only does it fail to be comprehensive, but it places the center of our faith in entirely the wrong location.

Along the same lines, "not Catholic" is not a good definition of "Protestant." It may have been the functional, and perhaps the only, definition of "Protestant" during the very early Reformation period, before the full development of Protestant theology. However, now that Protestantism has developed into a mature theological system, it must realize the damage it has caused by continuing to locate "not Catholic" so close to the center of its identity.

Perhaps the most destructive outcome has been the necessity for Protestants to continue to define Catholicism in terms that are no longer accurate and perhaps never were. For Protestants to continue to define themselves as "not Catholic" and yet continue to retain control over what that definition entails, they must also create a definition of "Catholic" to show what they are not.

As a matter of fact, to return to the analogy of Arianism discussed above, it is a well-known problem that the beliefs of Arians are largely unknown to us, as our definition of "Arian" comes primarily from advocates of the orthodox position, which elucidates Arianism only to say, "We are not this." The original

Arian writings have almost all been lost or destroyed; all that is left to us is the picture painted by their opponents, which may well be a caricature.

When we must either be completely correct or else cease to exist, then when we are wrong, we will often choose to ignore our error and continue to exist rather than sacrifice our identity to pursue the correction of the error.

While the Arians have died out, Catholicism is alive and well. Thus, for hundreds of years, Catholics have protested, "We also believe that God's grace alone is the basis for our salvation," and Protestants have responded, essentially, "Oh, no, you don't." In fact, Protestants must answer this way for Protestantism to persist in its current form. Because Protestants have defined themselves as "right" against a Catholic "wrong," if Catholicism is not actually "wrong," then Protestantism has just cause for an existential crisis.

An unbiased observer might remark that if we are to be unfortunately divided along denominational lines, then at least each denomination must have the right and responsibility to define its own beliefs in accordance with what it perceives the will of God to be, and we would agree. To depart from this basic principle and to force onto others definitions that do not fit them is to offend unnecessarily. In so doing, Protestants have placed obstacles between themselves and other believers that should, by all rights, not exist.

To retract these definitions, however, is to say, "We're sorry; we were wrong about you." "We were wrong" is a statement that, in a religious system built on correct doctrine as its *raison d'être* (not that this is, in reality, the case with Protestantism, but this is how conservative Five *Solae* Protestants have chosen to define themselves), cannot simply be an admission of error but must represent a direct challenge to the fundamental essence of one's own belief system. It raises difficult questions such as, "Why then do we exist as a separate, definable entity in the first place?"

Hopefully, we can see a core problem developing. If Protestantism is defined in such a way that an admission of error (and I mean error in a general sense; as stated above, *sola gratia* is not itself an unscriptural doctrine) amounts to a wholesale repudiation of the very rationale for its existence, then no actual errors will ever be admitted by Protestant organizational entities (denominations). When we must either be completely correct or else cease to exist, then when we are wrong, we will often choose to ignore our error and continue to exist rather than sacrifice our identity to pursue the correction of the error.

Of course, this situation cannot persist forever. Protestantism's fundamental errors and misunderstandings ("Catholics are legalists who do not believe that they are saved by grace") have become more obvious to each successive generation of Protestants, each of which has found itself in the presence of ever-increasing access to information, cross-denominational dialogue, and interfaith dialogue, confronted with the choice to either persist in ignorance, persist in willful error, or renounce their identity. In response, these young Christians have increasingly chosen to leave mainline Protestant denominations in favor of non-denominational churches or non-religious lifestyles. Since the mid-twentieth century, Protestantism, on the whole, has been in decline, at least in America, while Catholicism has held steady.

Grace in Judaism

As we look at Jewish-Christian relations, it becomes clear very quickly that the Catholic Church has been the most progressive of any Christian denomination as it relates to the Jewish people. Recent popes have made declarations to the effect that Jewish people retain their covenant status before God, a stance that Five *Solae* Protestants generally have yet to embrace. Our discussion on definitions helps us understand why this is the case.

Protestants have defined themselves as "not Catholic" and, particularly in the case of *sola gratia*, "not legalist," in contradistinction to all other believers (who are then necessarily "legalists"). On the other hand, Catholicism's self-definition is "the holy, catholic, and apostolic church." In other words, Catholicism consciously defines itself based on what it believes itself to be (the continuation of the New Testament church) rather than on what it is not. It is hard to imagine a Catholic defining himself as "not Protestant."

An organization believing itself to be the holy, catholic, and apostolic church can change. It can admit errors, it can refine its theology, and it can consciously better itself. It has a firm awareness of its own self-identity that allows it to make these changes. Pre-Vatican II Catholicism and post-Vatican II Catholicism may look very different, but this shift has no necessary effect on the Catholic Church's self-conception or definition.

However, a Protestant who still defines himself as "not Catholic" or "not legalist" does not have this firm awareness or even a well-defined self-identity, however many words may appear in his doctrinal statement. Therefore, to begin changing words in the doctrinal statement leads directly to an existential crisis: "Who am I, if I don't believe this anymore?"

A Roman Catholic can roll with the punches as the Catholic Church gradually renews its relationship with the Jewish people because he believes that the church is *right* because of *what it is*, not that it is *what it is* because it is *right*. A theologically conservative Five *Solae* Protestant is more likely to abandon his denomination if it begins to reassess its beliefs in this area or any area because his attitude toward the organization itself is fundamentally the opposite of the Catholic parishioner's attitude toward the Catholic Church.

However, to continue to persist in seeing himself as "not legalist" in contradistinction to Catholic and Jewish legalism, the Protestant must define not only Catholicism but Judaism as well. Protestantism's definition of Judaism has historically been just as unwarranted as the definition applied to Roman Catholics.

Five *Solae* Protestantism sees Judaism, as much as Catholicism, as its antithesis. If Protestants rely solely on grace, they believe, Jews are entirely dependent on their ability to follow the Torah. In Protestant thought the Jewish conception of God is that of John Bunyan's Moses as described in *Pilgrim's Progress*: "He spareth none; neither knoweth he how to shew mercy to those that transgress the law."

Therefore, *sola gratia* says both, "We are not legalists, as Catholics are," and, "We are not legalists, as Jews are."

However, like Catholics and unlike Arians, the Jewish people persist. In the last century especially, Jewish scholars have voiced fierce opposition to the Christian caricature of Judaism as graceless legalism.

These corrective voices went largely unheard until the publication of E.P. Sanders' *Paul and Palestinian Judaism* in 1977. His study is now a well-known benchmark in American New Testament studies and is perhaps one of the most influential Protestant monographs of the twentieth century.

Sanders quoted Solomon Schechter's *Some Aspects of Rabbinic Theology* to illustrate the problem:

> Either the theology of the Rabbis must be wrong, its conception of God debasing, its leading motives materialistic and coarse, and its teachers lacking in enthusiasm and spirituality, or the Apostle to the Gentiles is quite unintelligible.[48]

Sanders further noted that another Jewish scholar, Claude Montefiore, had similar reservations:

> Things were by no means so bad as Paul, in his pessimism, supposed. There was some righteousness and happiness in the world, as well as much misery and sin. And even from sin and misery there was a way out. That way was constructed by God's forgiveness and man's repentance. Its outward symbol was the Day of Atonement. What neither God nor man could do according to Paul except by the incarnation of the Son, was done according to Rabbinic Judaism constantly, hour by hour, and year by year. Nothing is more peculiar in the great Epistles than the almost complete omission of the twin Rabbinic ideas of repentance and forgiveness.[49]

A few Christian scholars began to open their ears to these voices in the early to mid-twentieth century. George Foot Moore admitted that Paul's seeming ignorance of Judaism's teachings about God's gracious impulse to forgive repentant sinners "seems from the Jewish point of view inexplicable."[50] It wasn't until Sanders that a Protestant scholar undertook a full study of Second Temple Judaism and found that Jesus' and Paul's Jewish contemporaries *did* conceive of themselves as having a relationship with God predicated on grace and that the Protestant caricature had been wrong all along—or, if others had made overtures toward this thesis before (Moore as well as W.D. Davies), Sanders was at least the first to bring it to widespread attention.

Reevaluations of Paul came soon afterward; the objections to Paul on the part of Jewish scholars were in actuality objections to Protestant interpretations of Paul, which were in turn based on Protestantism's skewed view of Judaism.

While Sanders' thesis has found broad acceptance in the academic field of New Testament studies and spurred an ongoing debate about Paul's theology, it has not yet enjoyed any formative influence on Protestant self-identity, nor has it found its way into conservative Five *Solae* Protestantism at all. The academic wing of conservative Protestantism, in fact, released a two-volume collection of essays attempting to disprove Sanders' thesis—in other words, to prove that the legalistic Judaism of Protestant theology was alive and well during the Second Temple Period.[51] Why have these scholars gone to such great lengths to disprove Sanders? Because legalistic Judaism needs to exist for conservative Protestants to know who they are and why they exist.

Rather than remark on the detailed exegetical work done by both Sanders and the contributors to *Justification and Variegated Nomism*, we might take a step back and consider the question again: Who has the right to define Judaism? We would argue that practitioners of Judaism must be allowed to define it—and if not Second Temple Judaism, then at least modern Judaism must be understood on the terms of its adherents and not on the terms of Protestant theology.

To continue to uphold *sola gratia* as a distinctive Protestant belief is to continue to denigrate Judaism as a graceless religion, and, as we have seen, religious Jewish scholars have rejected this definition. It is important to realize that the issue at hand is not one of being right or wrong but about the unfortunate willingness of Protestants to press their own definitions, terminologies, and categories onto other faith systems. It is impossible to unilaterally tell someone else what they believe and to be correct; to know the other, we must listen to the other.

The Centrality of Grace

Sola gratia can continue as a Protestant distinctive only as long as traditional Protestant theology continues to base its self-definition on an incorrect definition of other faiths—namely, Catholicism and Judaism. This is not to say that *sola gratia* is wrong, however. In fact, it may have the potential to be a great unifying factor in Judaism and Christianity.

To realize that *sola gratia* is inherent in Judaism helps us see grace in many of God's actions that, in traditional Protestant thought, have not been considered gracious. For example, the statement of faith of the Union of Messianic Jewish Congregations contains the following:

> God chose Israel, the Jewish people, and entered into
> an everlasting covenant with them so they might be

the firstfruits of a renewed humanity, who would mediate blessing and restoration to all the nations of the world. In gracious love, God gave to Israel the holy Torah as a covenantal way of life, and the holy Land of Israel as an inheritance and pledge of the blessing of the World to Come.[52]

To realize that sola gratia *is inherent in Judaism helps us see grace in many of God's actions that, in traditional Protestant thought, have not been considered gracious.*

Here a Jewish organization centered on Jesus provides a truly Jewish conception of the Torah: a gift given "in gracious love." Rather than, as Reformed theology might indicate, enslaving his people under a "covenant of works" resulting in condemnation and death,[53] God's relationship with the Jewish people is characterized by grace *even in the creation of the Sinai covenant.*

In truth, we *must* understand it this way in light of God's covenant with Abraham:

> I have made you the father of a multitude of nations. I will make you exceedingly fruitful, and I will make you into nations, and kings shall come from you. And I will establish my covenant between me and you and your offspring after you throughout their generations for an everlasting covenant, to be God to you and to your offspring after you. And I will give to you and to your offspring after you the land of your

sojournings, all the land of Canaan, for an everlasting possession, and I will be their God. (Genesis 17:5–8)

This unconditional promise, in which God swore to Abraham that he would always be the God of Abraham's descendants, is rooted in grace, and, as Sanders argued, the Jewish people have always generally understood that this gracious impulse has formed the basis for their entire relationship with God. So, whether in the giving of the Torah, the giving of the land of Israel, the establishment of the monarchy, or even the initiation of the exile, God's grace to the Jewish people underpins his every interaction with them.

Perhaps nowhere is this grace more apparent than in Jeremiah 31 and Ezekiel 36, in which God unconditionally promises to restore the Jewish people and permanently end their exile, whatever may come.

I would argue that if we go even further back, all the way to Genesis 1, God's creative impulse was also motivated essentially by grace. God did not need a physical creation; it could not offer him anything. Nor did he have any need to create sentient, willful beings in the form of the human race. In fact, for an infinite God to choose to create something finite is an inherently self-limiting act—out of infinite possibilities, God has (as far as we know) restricted himself to the existence of this current reality. Again, with each covenant he made, he restricted himself to abide by the promises he gave, first to the Jewish people and then to those from the nations of the world who attach themselves to Jesus.

Self-limitation for the sole benefit of another—in this case, the initiation of our existence and the forbearance to allow us to continue our existence in an imperfect state with the possibility of redemption and reconciliation—is gracious. God did not need to do these things, but he did them anyway. Grace lies at the heart of God's interaction with man on every level.

Even in the theme of judgment lies grace. Consider again Jesus' rendition of the final judgment:

> Then he will say to those on his left, "Depart from me, you cursed, into the eternal fire prepared for the devil and his angels. For I was hungry and you gave me no food, I was thirsty and you gave me no drink, I was a stranger and you did not welcome me, naked and you did not clothe me, sick and in prison and you did not visit me." Then they also will answer, saying, "Lord, when did we see you hungry or thirsty or a stranger or naked or sick or in prison, and did not minister to you?" Then he will answer them, saying, "Truly, I say to you, as you did not do it to one of the least of these, you did not do it to me." And these will go away into eternal punishment, but the righteous into eternal life. (Matthew 25:41-46)

Those who are to be judged unfavorably are sent "away into eternal punishment," an act seemingly devoid of grace. However, the reason for their condemnation is essentially their *failure to show grace to others*. Grace is tied so closely to the essential nature of God that his creatures, gracious as his disposition toward them might be, cannot coexist with him if they are not willing to extend grace toward others. This same motif is found in Matthew 6:14-15: "If you forgive others their trespasses, your heavenly Father will also forgive you, but if you do not forgive others their trespasses, neither will your Father forgive your trespasses."

> *Grace is tied so closely to the essential nature of God that his creatures, gracious as his disposition toward them might be, cannot coexist with him if they are not willing to extend grace toward others.*

So yes, *sola gratia*. It is by God's grace that we were created, that we are allowed to exist, and that we are saved. Our lives should mirror this grace and reflect it to the creation around us. As we have been forgiven, we must forgive; as we have been provided for, we must provide for others.

Conclusion

Lest this book be interpreted as nothing more than a thesis on "Where Luther Went Wrong," let us reaffirm that *sola gratia* is indeed an important concept as we seek to understand God's character and his relationship to the human race. However, when used as an instrument of religious elitism, *sola gratia* becomes a barrier and a source of misunderstanding.

Messianic Jewish theology will, of course, see the grace of God underlying his relationship with the Jewish people and with the nations. Nevertheless, this theology of grace does not require the foil of "legalistic" Judaism for its own self-definition. Instead, God's grace is seen throughout the Scripture as it records God's continuing relationship with the Jewish people.

Messianic Jews have an opportunity to demonstrate the grace inherent in Judaism through lives characterized by the extension of this grace to others. There is perhaps no better way to communicate an accurate conception of Judaism to traditional Protestants than to infuse Messianic Jewish life with grace. I think that all Messianic Jews would agree that the rigor of a life defined by the Torah can and should be married with grace and that such a visible expression of law and grace together has the potential to send a powerful message to those who continue to believe that Judaism is essentially a graceless religion.

This grace can be communicated in many ways: through acts of kindness, through the infusion of evenhandedness and openness into theological discourse, and through opening the doors of congregations and synagogues to curious outsiders, among others. If Messianic Jews strive to make the grace inherent in Messianic Judaism more visible and tangible in Messianic Jewish congregational life, it will be more and more impossible for people to claim that a life directed by the Torah is a life devoid of grace.

In this way, the traditional Protestant error of "Jewish legalism" can be corrected in what is itself a gracious manner—through humbly living by example.

Perhaps then, through grace properly lived out, we will begin to see the fruits of reconciliation—both between believers of different theological persuasions and between Jews and Christians. For, in the end, the kingdom of heaven will demand reconciliation; though it encompasses distinction, it allows no division.

Chapter Six

SOLUS CHRISTUS

Solus Christus is the fourth of the Five *Solae*—five Latin phrases that summed up the sixteenth-century Protestant Reformers' self-definition in contrast to certain doctrines of the Catholic Church and that continue to shape Protestant theology today.

Solus Christus represents an attempt to center the concepts of atonement, forgiveness, and justification on the person and work of Jesus Christ. Knowing only this, we are inclined to accept *solus Christus* uncritically; on the surface, it is unassailable. After all, what might we add to the work of Christ? Who could argue that God's grace is given to us on some other basis than Christ's atoning work?

If this were all the meaning the Reformers and their modern-day successors imputed to the phrase *solus Christus*, we could indeed accept it with no further discussion. However, as with the other *Solae*, we must dig a little deeper to see *solus Christus* in its historical context: as a polemical statement against the Catholic Church. In this context *solus Christus* communicates that salvation is through Christ *as opposed to* the sacraments and clerical apparatus of the Catholic Church.

It is common to see Protestants point to various Catholic practices—the veneration and invocation of Mary and the saints, the critical role of the sacraments, the mediatory role of priests—and claim that these usurp the role of Christ. In this sense *solus Christus*, like the other *Solae*, is as much a negative statement as a positive one: salvation is found in Christ *alone*, not in Mary, not in saints, not in sacraments, not in works, not in priests, and not in the Catholic Church. With *sola fide* and *sola gratia*, *solus Christus* excludes the "works" of Catholicism from any salvific role in the life of the believer. By grace alone, through faith alone, in Christ alone, the Christian is saved.

However, as we found in our discussion of *sola gratia*, Catholic theology is almost always more nuanced than Protestants tend to give it credit for. To wit, *solus Christus*, defined as salvation in Christ alone, is the official doctrinal position of the Catholic Church, as stated in the *Joint Declaration on the Doctrine of Justification*, which reads in part, "Through Christ alone are we justified when we receive this salvation in faith."[54] Catholics do not believe that sacraments save them; rather, they are saved by the grace of God in Christ, which is communicated to the believer through the sacraments.

As Thomas Aquinas put it, "God's grace is a sufficient cause of man's salvation. But God gives grace to man in a way which is suitable to him. Hence it is that man needs the sacraments that he may obtain grace."[55]

To Protestant ears, Aquinas' statement may still sound like works-based salvation—as if the sacraments have become, in Catholic theology, a sort of price put on something that has been freely given and should be freely received. Protestants are adamant that truly free grace should require no "works" on the part of human beings in order to receive it; if some work or action is required, grace is no longer free.

An allegory might be apt here. Imagine a parallel universe in which God has instituted a slightly different economy of salvation. In this imaginary universe, Christ's atoning death is still the only basis for salvation, but having access to this salvation is not predicated on saying a prayer, participating in sacraments (including baptism), or any of the other familiar methods that Christians have historically deemed appropriate to gain access to the unearned grace of God. Instead, one must pull a specific lever located somewhere on the earth. Let's say that one must pull the lever in faith; that is, one must believe that God's grace in Christ will be available to him only if he responds to God's call to pull this specific lever.

If this condition is met, then as soon as one pulls the lever, that person is granted free and unfettered access to the grace of God in Christ. The atoning death and victorious resurrection of Jesus ensure eternal life for everyone who pulls the lever.

In this parallel universe, is salvation in Christ alone? Or is salvation in Christ plus a lever?

What role does the lever play in salvation? Does it have saving power? Does pulling the lever constitute a "work" by which a person is saved? Does God somehow compensate the lever puller for his pulling of the lever? Is he saved by his pulling? Or by Christ?

Does the lever have any inherent significance? Does it actually communicate God's grace to its puller? Or does the act of pulling the lever only signify a deeper level of faith and commitment to which God is actually responding as he extends his grace to the lever puller?

While we will not attempt to answer all these questions, it should be clear to us that in Protestant theology the equivalent of the lever is the believer's relationship with Christ. Whether we term it accepting Christ, following Christ, giving one's life to Christ, becoming a disciple of Christ, or something else, our access to the grace of God hinges on our decision to enter into a relationship with Christ.[56]

A Protestant describing Catholic theology might be tempted to place all sorts of different things in the position of the fictional lever from our parallel universe. In particular, the sacraments would be a popular choice. The Catholic must continually participate in rituals to access God's grace. We might say that the Catholic must never stop pulling levers, pushing buttons, entering passwords, and so forth, to be saved, whereas the Protestant must only pull the lever once and be assured of salvation forever. On this basis, Catholics are accused of replacing the free grace available through Christ's atoning death with an expensive grace, a grace that is not really grace because it is paid for by a myriad of human works.

In either situation, because of the curious rules of our parallel universe, what we substitute for the lever is a moot point. It is silly to think that God would somehow reward a lever puller with eternal life merely for the act of pulling. Pulling a lever has no intrinsic value; its only significance is that which God has arbitrarily (we might even say, whimsically) assigned it. Pulling a lever in itself does nothing to make up for our numerous trespasses; what scant merit lies in this simple act of faith surely fails to fully make up the vast distance that still lies between the sinner and the righteous standard to which God holds his creation.

In short, the gift of eternal life seems a disproportionate response to the pulling of a lever. Of course, it is. However, the same logic holds if we replace the lever with the utterance of the "sinner's prayer" or even with a committed life of discipleship.

To these as well, the gift of eternal life seems a disproportionate response. Hence, *sola gratia*—by grace alone are we saved.

But what about the sacraments? Do Catholics believe that the practices of baptism, penance, and the Eucharist are somehow sufficient to merit salvation? Of course not. Any Catholic would agree that the gift of eternal life seems a disproportionate response to these simple acts of faith, obedience, and devotion. Hence, in Catholic theology, the sacraments are merely vehicles that God has chosen to communicate his grace to his people—grace that is available to begin with only because of the atoning work of Christ.

Whether one pulls a lever, says a penitential prayer, or participates in sacraments, he does not earn salvation, nor does he attain it through any other means than the grace of God, which has been made freely available through Christ's atoning death. Catholics believe this, and Protestants believe this. The problem is that so many Protestants do not believe that Catholics believe this, and here we find another misunderstanding occasioned by the nonexistence of interfaith dialogue in more conservative Protestant circles: We have defined ourselves against an "other" that does not exist except in the caricatures we draw.

To reiterate, if we set aside the strict monergism promulgated by Reformed theologians, most Christians believe that one must do *something* to become a Christian. This may be as simple as "accepting Christ" as one's Lord and Savior. But this is still *something*—there is still an expectation that one must perform some act, even if only an act of will, to receive the grace that is available in Christ alone.

If those of us who are Jesus' disciples were not required to undertake some discernable act of reception, some inward or outward profession of faith, then we could believe that all people everywhere will be saved. After all, none of us deserves salvation, and Christ's atoning work certainly avails sufficient grace to save as many as God chooses to save. The difference between those who are saved and those who are not is not a matter of personal merit—but of whether one has *access* to God's grace, which is freely given yet available only in Christ. Whether one believes that this grace is accessed through believing a doctrine, making a commitment to discipleship, saying a prayer, or participating in the sacraments, the ultimate legal basis for our salvation—Christ's atoning work—is the same.

Polity

Though it is primarily a statement of theology, *solus Christus* is specifically aimed to counter the professed role of the Catholic Church in general and priests in particular in their role as ministers of the seven sacraments—as mediators between the Catholic parishioner and God. The Reformers rejected this traditional role, believing instead that Christ is the only mediator between God and man. In this paradigm all believers are "priests"—all believers have equal access to the heavenly throne. This doctrine is widely known as the "priesthood of all believers."

Perhaps the most obvious consequence of this theological dichotomy between Catholics and Protestants can be seen in the sacrament of penance. Catholics find a biblical basis for the priestly administration of this sacrament in Jesus' statement in Matthew 16:19, which reads, "I will give you the keys of the kingdom of heaven, and whatever you bind on earth shall be bound in heaven, and whatever you loose on earth shall be loosed in heaven," and in another statement in John 20:23: "If you forgive the sins of any, they are forgiven them; if you withhold forgiveness from any, it is withheld."

> *After all, none of us deserves salvation, and Christ's atoning work certainly avails sufficient grace to save as many as God chooses to save.*

In Catholic theology these verses are interpreted within the context of apostolic succession—the idea that the authority of the apostles continues to reside in the episcopate, the modern-day successor to the original Apostolic College. As such, the episcopate has been granted the authority to communicate the forgiveness of sins to Catholic parishioners.

Apostolic succession thus forms the theological foundation for the doctrine that a Catholic priest, in his capacity as a divinely ordained mediator, has the authority to grant absolution to a penitent Catholic who undertakes the sacrament of penance.

Protestants, however, since the days of Luther himself, have rejected the idea that the authority of the apostles resides in the Catholic episcopate. This has, in turn, led to a much looser interpretation of Jesus' statements that appear to grant the power of absolution to the apostles. Protestants believe that forgiveness comes directly from Christ and not through the agency of any other mediator. While Protestants certainly believe that confession is an important part of Christian discipleship, they generally hold that one may confess his sins to any other believer in Jesus.

The Catholic interpretation of Jesus' delegation of authority to his apostles indeed seems incompatible with a Messianic

Jewish perspective. D.T. Lancaster has proposed a far more Jewish interpretation of Jesus' statements referenced above: that Jesus instead incorporated his apostles into a *beit din*—a sort of Jewish religious court that could resolve disputes and adjudicate issues of halacha for its own community. Messianic Jews almost universally assert that Jesus and the apostles operated within a completely Jewish cultural and theological framework; in this paradigm, Lancaster's view is certainly preferable to the idea that Jesus instituted "a sacramental system or hierarchical clerical status."[57]

This freedom to dissociate carries over to any church or denominational organization; if all believers are priests, then any believer can freely start his own church or denomination.

Even though the Reformers' theological basis for the rejection of the Catholic priesthood appears to be sound, it is interesting to see the implications of this rejection for Protestant polity. While *solus Christus* is certainly a statement of theology—and specifically, ecclesiology, so far as it makes a clear statement on the role and authority of the church and its appointed leaders—it is also a focused attack on the very institution of the Catholic Church. As we discussed in a previous chapter, the Catholic Church's self-identity is not predicated on its theology; Catholics are not Catholic because they are "right" or because they are doctrinally correct. Rather, the Catholic Church sees itself as *the* church;

its theological positions are in turn built on this strong sense of identity.

Solus Christus, by attacking the theological foundation of the roles of bishop and priest (and especially the role of the pope as the chief of the episcopate), is, of all the *Solae*, the one that most clearly attempts to undermine the self-conception, or core identity, of the Catholic Church. Whereas in Catholicism the episcopate has the final say in matters of faith and practice, in a fully realized Protestant theology this authority is spread equally among all believers. If one does not accept the authority of the Catholic episcopate, it follows that one may freely break with the Catholic Church; it is just another denomination, an ultimately human institution that may be differentiated from what many Protestants term the "invisible church." This freedom to dissociate carries over to any church or denominational organization; if all believers are priests, then any believer can freely start his own church or denomination.

A non-trivial ramification of *solus Christus* has been the flattening of the authority structure in many Protestant denominations and especially in non-denominational churches. The structure of the Catholic Church could be described as hierarchical or pyramidal in structure; the parish priest answers to a bishop, who in turn ultimately answers to the pope, the head of the episcopate. However, in those denominations or churches that take the priesthood of all believers to its most logical organizational end, the authority of the local pastor has instead been vested in him by the will of those in the congregation. His authority to shepherd the local church is not directly delegated to him by a higher organizational authority. Instead, the pastor's authority is sanctioned by the congregation, who, as "priests," function in place of an episcopate as the representation of God's authority on earth and who, in that capacity, are thought to mediate God's will to install the pastor as their spiritual leader. Note that in both polities, the authority of the pastor can be traced back to the authority of Christ to shepherd the church; the only difference is whether this authority is mediated through an episcopate or a congregational vote.

In truly congregational polity the pastor has no real spiritual authority that is not delegated to him by a majority vote of the members of his church. This is especially obvious when we note that congregational church constitutions usually provide means for a congregation to remove its pastor, an act unheard of in denominations that continue to embrace episcopal polity.

In reality, this extreme decentralization of authority is found only in the most strictly congregational churches, Baptists probably being the most visible example. Depending on whether one wishes to classify the Anglican Church as Protestant, various Protestant denominations range from fully hierarchical organizations with established episcopates separate from that of the Catholic Church all the way to congregational churches that operate as fully independent entities.

Denominations that trace their heritage back to the Anglican Church—most notably, the Methodists—tend toward more centralized leadership structures. Denominations that find their roots in the Reformed tradition, based on the teachings of John Calvin, tend to embrace an organizational structure based on elders, elected church leaders who together form regional and central governing bodies (usually called presbyteries and synods). In congregationalist denominations, such as the Southern Baptist Convention, there is no real central authority; these denominational structures are purposefully decentralized and granted very little authority in a direct *organizational* sense (though they often do their utmost to regulate the *theology* of their constituent churches). In all this diversity, it is still clear that the break from Catholicism has, in the vast majority of denominations, resulted in organizational structures that place far more weight on the authority of the individual believer and far less weight on the authority of the organization's central leadership.

It is not hard to see the parallel between the decentralization of authority in Protestantism and the decentralization of authority in Western civil government. The Catholic Church finds its origins in an age of kings and emperors, and its hierarchical system parallels that of an empire or monarchy. Protestantism, in turn, blossomed not too long before the monarchies of Western Europe began to give way to more democratic systems of government. We may also note that in societies that have instituted decentralized systems of civil government—America, for instance—those denominations and churches whose organizational structures are also decentralized have enjoyed massive growth. While one may not accept the existence of a causal link between the advent of Protestantism and the birth of modern Western democracy, these two movements certainly seem to share a common ideological foundation.[58]

One easily identifiable instance of ideological cross-pollination between congregational polity and American democracy can be found in the person of Roger Williams. Williams was an enemy of the state in Puritan Massachusetts; his rejection of any inherent authority belonging to the organizational church (which was at that time almost universally married to the state) was a key factor in his argument that civil governments must grant freedom of conscience and religion to their constituents.[59] The following century saw the adoption of these ideals by the founding fathers of the American system of government. To a large degree we have Williams—and by extension congregational polity rooted in *solus Christus*—to thank for the separation of church and state in America today.

While this may seem irrelevant to a discussion of *solus Christus*, it helps us to see the birth of Protestantism in a larger historical context—a context of rising literacy and education; greater cultural emphasis on the individual as opposed to the collective; and increasingly free promulgation of new ideas in philosophy, art, politics, and science in the Western world. Theological arguments aside, *solus Christus* fits very neatly into this cultural milieu.

Praxis

Before we return to the issue of polity, there are a few other interesting ramifications of *solus Christus*. One, in particular, has been the deprecation of the traditional role of saints—believers of outstanding holiness who, after their passing, are canonized by the Catholic Church. While a devout Catholic may invoke the name of a saint during prayer or ask a saint to offer prayers to God on his behalf, this practice is deprecated in Protestantism. Protestants believe that because Christ is the only mediator between God and man, prayers should be addressed to Christ (or to God, through Christ) alone; one cannot (or at least should not) address saints to intercede on his behalf.

It is interesting to note that a sort of parallel to the invocation of saints exists in Chasidic Judaism. Many Chasidim believe that their departed rebbes intercede on their behalf in the heavenly court. Breslover Chasidim gather to recite a specific prayer each year in Uman at the grave of Rabbi Nachman of Breslov, who famously claimed that he would save such penitents from *Gehinnom* (hell) by grabbing them by their *payot* (sidelocks).

In both Chasidism and Catholicism, these kinds of practices are justified by the belief that a very holy deceased person can offer prayers on behalf of the living in the same way that a very holy living person can offer intercessory prayer. It is telling that Protestants have no problem with intercessory prayer as such; Protestants have no compunction asking a friend to pray for them. At the same time, the practice of asking deceased saints to offer intercessory prayer is all but demonized in nearly all expressions of Protestantism. The real issue at hand seems to be whether it is permissible to contact the dead and not whether one may intercede in prayer on behalf of another. The role of Christ as the one mediator between God and man is not in question, as the Council of Trent made clear:

> They think impiously, who deny that the saints, who enjoy eternal happiness in heaven, are to be invoked; or who assert either that they do not pray for men; or, that the invocation of them to pray for each of us even in particular, is idolatry; or, that it is repugnant to the word of God; and is opposed to the honour of the *one mediator of God and men, Christ Jesus*.[60]

The fact that arguments concerning the invocation of saints frequently boil down to the issue of saints replacing Christ in his priestly role may reflect several factors: a fundamental misunderstanding on the part of Protestants of the invocation of saints in Catholic theology; abuses of this practice on the part of some Catholics; or, as we discussed in a previous chapter, a strong desire on the part of some Protestants to define Catholicism on their own terms to justify their theological position.

From a Messianic Jewish perspective, there is certainly a halachic issue with this practice as far as it appears to violate the prohibition of communicating with the dead (Deuteronomy 18:10–11). Roman Catholics get around this prohibition by appealing to the idea that the saints are alive in heaven and not dead, an idea difficult to reconcile with the traditional Jewish (and, by extension, Messianic Jewish) belief in a coming resurrection of the dead. While praying at cemeteries is common Jewish practice, Jewish halachic authorities are divided as to whether it is permissible for Jews to pray at cemeteries with the expectation that the departed will pray along with them; it is a contentious and nuanced topic. Because of this halachic difficulty, it seems unlikely that future generations of Messianic Jews will incorporate this practice in any form.

THE EARLY CHURCH

Though *solus Christus* is a statement of theology, its implications for church polity are most pressing. After all, if Catholics are correct that the episcopate is the divinely ordained successor of the Apostolic College, all Christians would be compelled to be Roman Catholic—regardless of whether the Catholic Church is strictly "correct" or biblical in the doctrinal positions it has espoused. In this light it is interesting to compare the various shifts in polity that find their roots in *solus Christus* with the polity of the early church. How does the early church compare, in an organizational sense, to the episcopal, Presbyterian, and congregational systems of church government?

It hardly needs to be said that all Christians believe that their church or denomination has a biblical polity in the sense that their polity is claimed to mirror that of the early church. Congregationalists point to, among other things, the first few verses of Acts 13, in which the Holy Spirit works through the local church—not through bishops or elders—to commission Paul and Barnabas to be missionaries. Presbyterians point to numerous verses that indicate the existence of multiple elders in any given local church (such as James 5:14) as well as to the practice of the laying on of hands by a body of elders to ordain new leaders (Acts 6:5–6) to support the existence of a sort of presbytery, or body of elders, in the early years of the church. Proponents of episcopal polity need only appeal to the supremacy of the apostles in the government of the early church to justify the existence of an authoritative episcopate at the top of the church's governing structure. They may also point to Paul's directions to Titus, which appear to imply that the elders of local churches are to be appointed by apostles or by their representatives (Titus 1:5).

Richard Bauckham, an eminent scholar on the early church and the role of the apostles, has made a strong case that the apostles, with James, the Lord's brother, at their head, were the unquestioned leaders of the early church.[61] The Gordian knot we must hack through as we compare different systems of polity to that of the early church presents itself as the physical absence of the apostles in today's church. If no person or group today has the right to claim the historical role of the Apostolic College as the overseers of the entire Christian church, how can any denomination justify emulating the apparently episcopal organizational structure of the early church?

At the same time, as we see how the decisive influence of the apostles kept the church on the right theological track, we are loathe to consider strict congregational polity as a satisfactory solution. Consider the Jerusalem Council, at which the apostles kept the church from requiring Gentile believers in Jesus to undergo ritual proselytization. We may wonder how the council would have turned out had everyone in the church gotten a vote. Even if all believers have access to the throne of God through Jesus Christ, the decision of the council is nowhere described as the result of a church-wide poll but as the result of debate among the apostles and elders in Jerusalem.

It should go without saying that as we try to compensate for the absence of the apostles, we must be careful not to let our civil political system dictate the structure of our churches. Christians who embrace Western democracy have a cultural bias toward establishing or joining organizations in which they have a direct or indirect influence on the decisions of the leadership. This model does not overlay well on the New Testament, in which apostles and elders—both, at least in the first decades of the church, positions of appointment—are consistently held up as the church's spiritual authority figures.

Comparative Religion

Those of us who have adopted a Messianic Jewish perspective are used to peeking over the fence at broader Judaism; in our context, it makes sense to examine Judaism's model of synagogue governance, if for no other reason than to get another reference point. What we find makes for an interesting comparison and contrast with the polities of various Christian denominations.

First, however, we must note that observant Jews share an interesting characteristic with the Catholic Church in that a

Jewish person is defined more by his sense of identity than by his belief system. One does not become a Jew by believing certain things. A Jewish person's sense of identity is rooted in a broad but defined stream of tradition; this stream of tradition, in turn, informs the belief and practice of the observant Jew. This relationship between identity, tradition, belief, and practice is closer to the Catholic paradigm than to the Protestant, in which one's identity hinges more directly on one's belief system.

> *This model does not overlay well on the New Testament, in which apostles and elders—both, at least in the first decades of the church, positions of appointment—are consistently held up as the church's spiritual authority figures.*

Historically speaking, the religious organizational structure of Judaism had an important similarity to that of the Catholic Church in the sense that there was one adjudicating body—the Sanhedrin—that was above all others in its authority to adjudicate matters of religious practice. When the Sanhedrin still existed, it functioned as the final arbiter in issues of praxis, not unlike the Catholic episcopate. We see this structure mirrored in the early church, with the apostles having the final authority of adjudication within the Jesus-believing community. The apostles comprised a *beit din*, or a group of judges, functionally comparable to the Sanhedrin itself in that there was no higher earthly authority to which a member of the Jesus community could appeal.[62]

However, after the dissolution of the Sanhedrin, Judaism was forced to adapt in a practical sense to its absence. This adaptation did not see the authority of the Sanhedrin diluted or passed on to another body. Today there is no universally accepted single authority figure or body of adjudicators to which all Jews, or even Orthodox Jews, are compelled to answer. The absence of the Sanhedrin has created a vacuum that may be compared to the absence of the apostles or an equivalent episcopate in Protestant denominations and independent churches.

Knowing this, it is astonishing to see how well Judaism has held together over the past fifteen hundred years, though as in Protestantism, there have been major schisms in Judaism. Within the Orthodox community are various sects of Chasidim, Haredi, Modern Orthodox, and others. Since the Haskalah (the Jewish Enlightenment) of the eighteenth and nineteenth centuries, other expressions of Judaism have also arisen—Reform, Conservative, Reconstructionist, and so forth; some of these movements have deviated so far from traditional Judaism that it is difficult to consider them all together.

However, at least within Orthodox Judaism, there remains an authoritative body of tradition to which all Jews are expected to defer. Also, certain figures have emerged whose words are given great weight in matters of faith and practice. Many of these men were controversial in their own day, but over time a consensus has arisen within the entire Jewish community around these men and their writings. Yosef Karo's *Shulchan Aruch*, the writings of Maimonides, and Rashi's commentaries on the Torah and the Talmud are among those works that have become almost universally accepted within the Orthodox Jewish community as guideposts for interpretation, doctrine, and practice. In modern times certain *poskim*—men who decide issues of halacha in unprecedented situations—are likewise looked to as defining voices beyond their own local communities. The late Moshe Feinstein is an example of such a *posek*; his decisions are widely considered as benchmarks by the broader Orthodox Jewish community.

However, in the midst of this apparent consensus, there is seemingly always room for discussion, debate, and disagreement. Even the most distinguished *poskim* have made decisions that are not accepted by the rest of the Jewish community. No single person or group of people has that kind of authority. This is at least part of the reason why observant Jews throughout history have repeatedly attempted to reestablish the Sanhedrin; from a halachic perspective, there is simply no suitable replacement for it.

Despite the disadvantage presented by the absence of a Sanhedrin, local synagogues gain great flexibility from Orthodox Judaism's current organizational structure while still retaining a solid identity as part of a defined movement. Local rabbis, widely recognized *poskim*, and the body of historical Jewish tradition all come together to create an environment in which local synagogues have the power and freedom to deal with matters unique to their community while still being easily recognizable (and mutually recognized) parts of a much larger movement. The resilience of Orthodox Judaism even through the Haskalah and into the modern era certainly owes much to this flexible yet firm organizational structure.

Messianic Jewish Polity

Owing to its roots in evangelical Protestantism, Messianic Judaism today tends congregational polity. Most Messianic congregational leaders feel the same freedom to dissociate that compelled Luther to break with the Roman Catholic Church; this freedom often manifests as a resistance toward denominational structures of any kind. While there are a few Messianic Jewish denominations, membership in denominational organizations is hardly a defining characteristic of Messianic congregations. The two Messianic Jewish denominations that have gained the broadest recognition, the IAMCS and the UMJC,[63] currently encompass a combined total of 217 synagogues, and while no concrete numbers exist, some estimates place the total number of Messianic synagogues as high as eight hundred worldwide,[64] a number that does not include a countless conglomeration of house congregations.

Both the IAMCS and the UMJC are led by competent, qualified, and respected individuals. However, the organizational reality these individuals must deal with is understandably messy. Not just outside these denominations but within them as well, individual Messianic congregations fall in very different places on an extraordinarily wide spectrum. The idea of the priesthood of all believers, with its theological foundation in *solus Christus*, provides a sort of license for this wide variation in praxis; the leaders of most Messianic synagogues do not feel beholden to the decisions of any particular rabbi or organization outside their local communities. It goes without saying that more disconnected synagogues and house congregations feature an even wider range of beliefs and practices, many of which are questionable as far as their value and authenticity in a truly Jewish context.

However, we may expect—and enthusiastically await—a more mature phase to come as Messianic Judaism continues to grow. Through the efforts of organizations like the UMJC, the MJRC, and the MJTI,[65] one can imagine Messianic Jews embracing a voluntary centralization comparable to that seen in Orthodox Judaism. While Messianic congregations are likely to remain organizationally independent (just as many Orthodox synagogues are), the broader Messianic community would have much to gain by identifying strong and respectable voices in its midst and by deferring to these voices in a manner similar to the way Orthodox Jews defer to their own *poskim*.

It would be difficult for most local Messianic synagogues to give up the theological and practical autonomy that comes with complete independence. However, this independence comes at a price—namely, schism and infighting; Protestantism has paid this price dearly over the past five hundred years. Far from a single movement away from the Roman Catholic Church, Protestantism as a whole has been fractured beyond repair. It has been rightly said that Protestants organize their firing squads in circles.

It is true that the eclectic soup of Protestantism created an environment in which Messianic Judaism has been free to establish its unique identity; it is relatively easy to tolerate one more expression of discipleship to Jesus among so many that are already so varied. However, Messianic Judaism itself has little to gain in the long term by mirroring Protestantism in this regard. It may be wiser to cultivate an environment closer to that of Orthodox Judaism in which debate, discussion, and disagreement are accepted within defined parameters yet in which a degree of deference is granted to those voices, both historical and modern, that have had a significant role in shaping the identity and theology of Messianic Judaism. This would represent a great step toward the important hallmarks of mutual recognition, common tradition, and organizational flexibility that helped Orthodox Judaism weather the storm of the Enlightenment.

Truly all believers in Jesus have access to the throne of God directly through him—through our Master, Yeshua, who intercedes for us.

Though the kind of environment I have described is still certainly loosely structured in an organizational sense, diehard congregationalists may still object to it. The theological impetus for this objection goes something like this: *Solus Christus*—salvation is in Christ alone; therefore, all believers are priests—congregational leaders answer to Christ alone and not to the titular leaders of an organization or denomination; therefore, a local congregational leader's interpretation, opinion, doctrine, teaching, or practice is theoretically no more and no less important or valid than anyone else's.

However, while we should certainly embrace the doctrine that all believers in Jesus have access to God through Christ alone, it does not necessarily follow that the best organizational model for Messianic synagogues is one based on strictly congregational polity. There is simply too much to lose by favoring the individual congregation at the expense of the broader movement. If individual Messianic Jews and congregational leaders could identify voices worth rallying around, they could bring a sense of unity to Messianic Judaism far surpassing that which it currently enjoys. On the heels of unity would come clarity, definition, and resilience—foundation stones for a Messianic Judaism that will stand the test of time in the same way, and for the same reasons, that Orthodox Judaism has survived and thrived.

Conclusion

As for *solus Christus*, the simple idea that salvation is available only through the work of Christ is certainly a foundational doctrine for any believer, Jew or Gentile. Furthermore, the clerical system instituted by the church in the patristic era does not do justice to Jesus' teaching once he is seen in his first-century Jewish context. Truly all believers in Jesus have access to the throne of God directly through him—through our Master, Yeshua, who intercedes for us.

At the same time, however, this belief does not necessarily lead us to the conclusion that Messianic Jewish polity should mirror that of any particular Protestant expression. While congregationalist Protestants find justification for their polity in *solus Christus*, this conclusion is not logically or theologically sound enough for us to accept uncritically. It may be wiser for a maturing Messianic movement to look toward a more Jewish organizational structure—a structure that is still messy in an organizational sense but has a clear identity through common tradition, mutual recognition, and a degree of deference to widely respected and recognized leaders.

Certainly, many Messianic Jewish leaders have taken important steps toward unity, cohesion, and the development of an authentically Jewish expression of discipleship to Yeshua. The organizations mentioned above, publications such as *Kesher* and *Messiah Journal*, and conferences such as Hashivenu and the

Borough Park Symposium have all become indispensable forums for Messianic Jewish dialogue. I don't intend to deprecate the efforts of those who have poured their lives into making these forums possible or adding their voices to the ongoing discussion. On the contrary, my appeal is directed to those who have resisted establishing connections with these forums.

The more isolated—the more independent, the more strictly "congregational"—Messianic Jewish congregations choose to be, the longer the road becomes toward building a movement that can be taken seriously on the world stage. If more Messianic congregations were to establish formal relationships with grounded Messianic Jewish organizations and join their voices with the ongoing discussion rather than continuing to sound the trumpet in isolation, Messianic Judaism as a whole would take a necessary step toward earning the trust and respect this movement deserves and desperately needs if it is to fulfill its historical and biblical role as a recognized bridge between Christianity and Judaism.

CHAPTER SEVEN

SOLI DEO GLORIA

The last of the Five *Solae*, and the subject of the final chapter in this book, is *soli Deo gloria*, which, loosely translated, states "to God alone [be the] glory." *Soli Deo gloria* has percolated into popular culture as J.S. Bach's favored subscription; it appears at the bottom of most of his scores. The modern phenomenon of performance artists thanking or praising God for their success is perhaps another tributary of this same stream.

Of all the *Solae*, *soli Deo gloria* is the most difficult to argue with. Who would steal God's glory? Who would dare? Are there really Christians who believe that God is not ultimately deserving of all glory?

If you have been following me closely, you might have already anticipated the answer: No, there are no Christians who believe that they or anyone else deserve a share of God's glory. All Christians believe in *soli Deo gloria*, at least when understood in these narrow terms.

Is *soli Deo gloria* simply a practical reminder to glorify God? Is it a rough Reformation-era equivalent to the 1990's "What would Jesus do?"—a personal mantra to help Christians remember to thank, praise, and glorify God in various types of circumstances?

As we have reviewed the other four *Solae*, we have noted that each of these statements was carefully developed for a specific purpose: to differentiate Protestantism from Roman Catholicism. They were designed to cut deeply, to create a divide between these two competing definitions of authentic Christianity. It is within this context that we will find the meaning of *soli Deo gloria*. We must ask, to what specifically were the Reformers objecting when they invoked the principle of *soli Deo gloria*?

In broad terms, the Reformers objected to the veneration of the saints, Mary, and the pope and other ecclesiastical leaders. Again, as with previous *Solae*, we are initially inclined to agree. No matter what greatness a person might attain, there can be no comparison with God's greatness; why then would we venerate the hierarchy of the Catholic Church?

This broad interpretation of *soli Deo gloria* brings to mind Luke's account of the death of Herod Agrippa, recorded in Acts 12:20–23:

> Herod was angry with the people of Tyre and Sidon, and they came to him with one accord, and having persuaded Blastus, the king's chamberlain, they asked for peace, because their country depended on the king's country for food. On an appointed day Herod put on his royal robes, took his seat upon the throne, and delivered an oration to them. And the people were shouting, "The voice of a god, and not of a man!" Immediately an angel of the Lord struck him down, because he did not give God the glory, and he was eaten by worms and breathed his last.

Surely when we fail to give God the glory, we tread the same dangerous ground upon which Herod met his end. The immediate death of this presumptuous would-be king serves as a chilling reminder of God's jealousy in all things concerning his glory.

Again, no Roman Catholic would dispute this fact.

> *The same word* kavod *can be used for a glory unique to God, as manifested in theophanies, but also simply of the honor due to kings and other authority figures in the ancient world.*

The question is not whether we believe God is deserving of all glory. The question is whether it is ever proper to praise or glorify a person—whether, in doing so, we detract from God's glory.

One answer might find support in Isaiah 42:8, in which God states through Isaiah, "I am the LORD; that is my name; my glory [Heb. *kavod*] I give to no other, nor my praise to carved idols." From this verse one might conclude that no other being deserves any *kavod* whatsoever. But does *kavod*, the word translated "glory" in this passage, embody the same concept to which the *gloria* in *soli Deo gloria* refers?

The answer is, it depends. The same word *kavod* can be used for a glory unique to God, as manifested in theophanies, but also simply of the honor due to kings and other authority figures in the ancient world.[66] If God's essential glory were all that is at stake, certainly all Christians (and, for that matter, observant Jews) stand on *soli Deo gloria*. But if *soli Deo gloria* is meant as anti-Catholic polemic, it seems the Reformers meant to invoke the latter definition—to say that God alone is due any and all kinds of honor—which raises several problems; at the very least, did not Paul press Romans to give honor to those to whom is due honor (Romans 13:7)?

The English "glory" comes to us more or less intact from the Latin *gloria*; we deal again with a multifaceted definition that depends on context. Certainly if by "glory" we mean "worship," glory may only be properly accorded to God. But if "glory" simply means "honor" or "credit" or "fame," then glory is commonly accorded to human beings throughout the Scriptures as well as throughout the daily life of every individual. A plaque on a statue, a bachelor's degree, the signature of an artist on a painting, a publisher's imprint, and a positive movie review are all claims to or conferrals of glory in this diminished sense. According to King Solomon, simply being wise is worthy of *kavod* (Proverbs 3:35). As we reach the level of the mundane, it becomes more and more difficult to see these instances as somehow detracting from the unique sort of honor that is due to God alone.

If *soli Deo gloria* is meant to refer only to God's unique glory, in a sense in which God alone is deserving of worshipful honor, then certainly all Christians—including Catholics—can affirm this doctrine. However, *soli Deo gloria* is not always invoked with this strict idea of glory in mind.

Overkill

As with previously discussed *Solae*, the way in which the doctrine of *soli Deo gloria* has been invoked in "pop" Christianity often unfortunately overshadows whatever specific idea the Reformers had in mind. My experience at conservative Christian colleges speaks to the fact that in more conservative Protestantism, it is not uncommon to see the idea of *soli Deo gloria* taken to a practical extreme. Anyone who honors another or allows himself to be honored risks being accused of stealing some of God's glory.

This tendency toward self-effacement fits into another common Protestant mindset in which, just as God can do no evil, humans can do no good. An unfortunate consequence of this mindset seems to be a "tall poppy syndrome" in which successful pastors, artists, and other Christians are verbally cut down simply for allowing others to enjoy and praise their work—as if each were a miniature Herod, a complete sinner stealing credit that rightfully belongs only to God.

Disdain for megachurches, popular Christian music and media, and success in general—i.e., a church that focuses on "numbers" (of baptisms—see Acts 2:41)—can all be cloaked by the veil of *soli Deo gloria*. For God to increase, we must decrease; we are not allowed to be famous or influential; only God is allowed these attributes.

Recall our assessment of *sola fide*, which will provide an interesting parallel: We asserted that rather than judging a person based on his decision to follow or not to follow Jesus, God's final judgment encompasses a whole person—who he became, what he did, what he amounted to. Those in Christ are transformed through the power of the Holy Spirit so that their final eschatological judgment is positive—they are good, both *de jure* and *de facto*. The good things that we do are in fact the works of Christ in us, and we glorify God through Christ for these works. But at the same time, the Scriptures themselves laud the one who undertakes good works, who is obedient, who makes wise decisions. Both human will and divine grace are at work when a disciple of Jesus does what is right; the Scriptures accord honor both to God, the source of righteousness, and to the good servant, the worker of righteousness (Matthew 25:14-30: "Well done, good and faithful servant").

The fear that by attempting good works (in the case of *sola fide*) or by taking credit for one's actions (in the case of *soli Deo gloria*) one infringes on God's domain is a characteristically Protestant fear. This fear rests on a very different construal of the concepts of faith and glory than one would find in Judaism or Catholicism. Ben Zoma, for example, advises those who seek honor (*kavod*, Isaiah's term for God's glory) not to give up their quest but to honor others to in turn be honored themselves.[67] Similarly, R. Yose promises the honor of others as a reward for honoring the Torah.[68] This approach to honor is, as the Protestant approach, somewhat counterintuitive; it is, however, apparent that these rabbis did not consider God's honor to be infringed by the one who seeks to be honored by others.

Similarly, Aquinas, invoking 1 Corinthians 2:12 and Matthew 5:16, wrote that the desire for glory—that is, the recognition of one's good—is not in itself sinful; rather, only the desire for vain or empty glory is sinful. Empty glory includes glory that is not ultimately referred to God; here Aquinas would agree with a strict interpretation of *soli Deo gloria*. This does not stop Aquinas from concluding that what is good in ourselves and others can and should be openly recognized as such.[69]

Saints

So what of the honor that the Catholic Church accords to its ecclesiastical hierarchy and to saints who have passed on?

If this honor is understood to be the honor due to one who has done well, who has lived admirably, then in honoring the righteous ones who have passed on, we stand in a biblical stream of thought. Consider how the Scriptures themselves laud Abraham, David, Paul, and other heroes among God's people. These extraordinary human beings are lifted up as examples despite their faults. The author of Hebrews is especially striking in his willingness to lift up biblical figures as heroic examples for his generation, exemplified in the famous eleventh chapter of his letter.

In all this we give God all glory; there is no contradiction once we understand that different forms of honor are appropriately given in different circumstances.

No less inspiring are the examples set by all those who have lived as outstanding disciples of Christ since the end of the Apostolic Era. To our detriment, we downplay or deprecate the righteous acts, wisdom, and legacy of great historical figures from the early church through the present day—from Polycarp the martyr to Francis of Assisi to Teresa of Calcutta—under the veil of theological disagreement. It would be better to give the righteous their due while still glorifying God for the good these men and women have accomplished.

If honor is understood to mean the honor due to those in positions of authority, then far be it from us to begrudge Roman Catholics the right to show honor to their ecclesiastical authorities. Just as most Protestants would not openly dishonor their pastors, we would expect Catholics to show honor to their priests and the higher authorities of the Catholic Church.

In all this we give God all glory; there is no contradiction once we understand that different forms of honor are appropriately given in different circumstances.

CONCLUSION

In considering the Five *Solae* from a Messianic Jewish perspective, we have at times questioned their usefulness—at least as they seem to be understood by today's evangelical Protestants. Before we conclude, it is worth reminding ourselves what benefit this analysis has and why it was undertaken to begin with.

It would be fair to say that modern Messianic Judaism can trace its heritage directly back to evangelical Protestantism. While there are self-consciously Jewish "Hebrew Catholics," and while some Messianic Jewish pioneers identified with other denominations not usually classified as evangelical (P.P. Levertoff was an Anglican priest), today both the organizational history of the major Messianic Jewish denominations and the individual theological heritage of most who identify themselves as Messianic Jews lie in nineteenth- and twentieth-century evangelical Protestantism.

Evangelicalism itself has changed much over that period, surviving as culture-weary "fundamentalism" through the secular 1920s and '30s, reemerging as "neo-evangelicalism" in the '40s and '50s, heavily engaging in politics in the '80s, and today dealing with fragmentation and reorganization as denominational lines blur and as a new generation emerges with new ideas about what it looks like to be a disciple of Jesus in the postmodern world.

Messianic Judaism has also changed; undertaking a conscious shift from "Hebrew Christianity" to "Messianic Judaism" about half a century ago, the leaders of the Messianic Jewish movement acted on a conscious desire to identify themselves as Jews practicing a form of their historical faith just as strongly as they identified as disciples of Jesus.

Today Messianic Judaism continues to face accusations of syncretism, perhaps the most common being that Messianic Judaism is merely evangelical Protestantism wearing a *tallit* and a *kippah*. Both mainstream Christians and observant Jews have good reasons for wanting to see Messianic Judaism as a Christian cake with Jewish icing.

Christians—not all, but many—desire to use Messianic Judaism as a side door to bring Jewish people into the normative mainstream church. Ultimately, the retention of Jewish identity among Messianic Jews is a dangerous departure from the historical teachings of the church regarding the Law and the Jewish people, and Messianic Jews are allowed to play with fire in this way only because of the missionary potential of the movement. Some Christians who have begun to understand the fundamental shift in self-conception from "Jewish Christian" to "Messianic Jew" have decried the movement on that very basis[70]—Judaism is still seen as fundamentally wrong, at best an outdated way of life and at worst a corporate error that Jesus came to correct.

Non-Jesus-believing Jews, on the other hand, have no historical reason to take seriously the claims of Messianic Jews that they are upholding Jewish identity and practice for any other reason than to convert Jews to Christianity. The church throughout history has unfortunately used Jewish identity and trappings as bait to lure Jewish people away from Judaism and away from their Jewish identity. While many Christians today have rejected these missionary tactics, the Jewish community has not forgotten them. Because Messianic Judaism doesn't look so very different from the "Judaism" dishonestly embraced by certain eighteenth- and nineteenth-century missionaries, it is all too easy to lump Messianic Judaism in with other Christian mission efforts. In doing so, observant Jews can easily absolve themselves of any responsibility to take Messianic Judaism seriously.

Messianic Judaism deserves a better reputation than it currently has in either mainstream Christianity or Judaism. Perhaps at various places and at various times it has been what its detractors believe it to be, but Messianic Judaism today is a growing and thriving movement, in many ways an authentic reconstruction of the theology and practice of the early church.

Several obstacles remain in the way if the goal of organizational Messianic Judaism is to be recognized as a truly Jewish and truly Yeshua-centered movement. One of these obstacles is a tendency that is perhaps not evident among highly educated Messianic Jewish scholars but is prevalent in many Messianic congregations: an uncritical acceptance of Reformation-era theology.

The academic foundation for the existence of Messianic Judaism as a movement—the foundation for the retention of Jewish theology and practice within the body of Messiah in contrast to the deprecation of Judaism in traditional Christian theology—exists in several streams of scholarship; namely, the Radical New Perspective on Paul and the Third Quest for the Historical Jesus. These schools of thought have laid an ax to traditional conceptions of first-century Judaism and the first-century Jesus movement. In doing so, they have cleared the way for Messianic Jews to boldly claim solidarity with Jesus and Paul while still unashamedly practicing Judaism. Yet when these same Messianic Jews—and Gentiles—hold on to those threads of anti-Catholic and anti-Jewish thought that are woven through the Five *Solae*, they risk undermining that very foundation. One cannot accept both the Jewish Paul of the Radical New Perspective and the Lutheran Paul who left Judaism behind on the road to Damascus.

> *One cannot accept both the Jewish Paul of the Radical New Perspective and the Lutheran Paul who left Judaism behind on the road to Damascus.*

It is contradictory to claim to live a Jewish life in Messiah and at the same time deprecate Jewish tradition (*sola scriptura*), minimize the importance of good works (*sola fide*), claim that traditional Judaism is legalistic (*sola gratia*), distance oneself from organizational Messianic Judaism (*solus Christus*), and refrain from giving honor to those who have gone before one, those on whose shoulders we all stand (*soli Deo gloria*). While all five *Solae* can be construed in such a way as to exclude these anti-Jewish and anti-Catholic tendencies, to do so is to remove something of their essence as anti-Jewish and anti-Catholic polemic.

It would be better for Messianic Judaism, a movement that arguably predates anything that can be usefully called Christianity, to plant its roots in theological ground more ancient than that of the Reformation. While only a fool would deny that we have much to learn from the Reformers, it is equally foolish to embrace a supposedly Messianic Jewish theology that is really only Protestantism with a thin veneer of Jewish practice. Messianic Jews and Gentiles do the latter at great risk to their ability to show Messiah in his true Jewish colors to the broader Jewish community from which he is currently estranged.

While developing a truly Messianic Jewish theology is hard work, it must be undertaken if this movement is to survive as an identifiably Jewish and Jesus-centered phenomenon.

ENDNOTES

1. Seth Godin, *Tribes: We Need You to Lead Us* (New York, NY: Portfolio, 2008), 11.
2. R. Kendall Soulen, *The God of Israel and Christian Theology* (Minneapolis, MN: Fortress, 1996), 25–56.
3. *Yeshua Matters: Putting the Jewish Rabbi Back at the Center of Christianity* (Marshfield, MO: FFOZ, 2015), *Israel Matters: Putting the Jewish People Back at the Center of God's Plan* (Marshfield, MO: FFOZ, 2015).
4. Christian Smith, *The Bible Made Impossible: Why Biblicism Is Not a Truly Evangelical Reading of Scripture* (Grand Rapids, MI: Brazos, 2011), ix.
5. Westminster Larger Catechism 4.
6. Smith, *Bible Made Impossible*, 3–54.
7. Richard N. Longenecker, *Biblical Exegesis in the Apostolic Period* (Grand Rapids, MI: Eerdmans, 1999).
8. See Magnus Zetterholm's *Approaches to Paul: A Student's Guide to Recent Scholarship* (Minneapolis, MN: Fortress, 2009) for an overview of some of these "Radical New Perspective" scholars.
9. Particularly relevant here is Kathy Ehrensperger, *Paul and the Dynamics of Power: Communication and Interaction in the Early Christ-Movement* (New York, NY: T&T Clark, 2009), 5–8.
10. Richard Bauckham, *Jude, 2 Peter* (vol. 50 of *Word Biblical Commentary*; Waco, TX: Word, 1983), 7.
11. *Messiah Magazine* 1 (Winter 2012).
12. Robert Jewett, *Romans* (*Hermeneia: A Historical and Critical Commentary on the Bible*; Minneapolis, MN: Fortress, 2006), 179.
13. Council of Trent, Canon XXIV.

14 Council of Trent, Canon XXXII.

15 Catholic Encyclopedia, s.v. "justification," [cited 30 August 2016]. Online: http://newadvent.org/cathen/08573a.htm.

16 Emphasis added. From the 1545 Luther Bibel [accessed 30 August 2016]. Online: http://www.biblegateway.com/passage/?search=romans%20 3:28&version=LUTH1545. Compare with the ESV's rendition of the verse: "For we hold that one is justified by faith apart from works of the law."

17 One of thousands of possible examples of this phenomenon is the text *Orthodoxy and Heresy* by Joel Parkinson (Shippensburg, PA: Companion, 1991), 40–41, in which Catholics are regarded as heretics for departing from the "orthodox" (Protestant) plan of salvation. Parkinson's text was at one time required reading for undergraduate religion students in the largest Christian university in the world.

18 Paul A. Rainbow, *The Way of Salvation: The Role of Christian Obedience in Justification* (Milton Keynes, England: Paternoster, 2005), xvii.

19 F.C. Baur, *Paul the Apostle of Jesus Christ: His Life and Work, His Epistles and His Doctrine* (ed. Eduard Zeller; trans. Rev. A. Menzies; London, England: Williams and Norgate, 1875), 2:297.

20 Rainbow, *Way of Salvation*, xvii.

21 John Calvin, *Calvin's Commentaries*, vol. 22 (ed. and trans. John Owen; Grand Rapids, MI: Baker, 2009), 315.

22 Baur, *Paul the Apostle*, 2:297–299.

23 Many of Baur's works reflect and reinforce this basic viewpoint, which held sway in German scholarship more or less through much of the nineteenth century. German theological scholarship in turn has enjoyed wide influence throughout the Western world.

24 Craig C. Hill, *Hellenists and Hebrews: Reappraising Division within the Earliest Church* (Minneapolis, MN: Fortress, 1992), 5–17, explores the continuation and maturation of this theme throughout history up to Martin Hengel. See also Scot McKnight, *The Letter of James* (The New International Commentary on the New Testament; Grand Rapids, MI: Eerdmans, 2011), 262 n. 147 for scholars who continue to read the letter of James as anti-Pauline polemic.

25 The preeminent expositor of this view is Richard Bauckham. See in particular his essay "James and the Jerusalem Church," in *The Book of*

      Acts in Its Palestinian Setting (ed. Richard Bauckham; vol. 4 of *The Book of Acts in Its First Century Setting*; Grand Rapids, MI: Eerdmans, 1995), 415–480.

26   Even some of the most conservative commentators are unashamed to take this view. F.F. Bruce speaks candidly of "Paul's increasing reservations about the Jerusalem Decree" and of the apostles' disapproval of "Paul's libertarian attitude" toward the Torah and Jewish customs in *Paul, Apostle of the Heart Set Free* (Grand Rapids, MI: Eerdmans, 1977), 347–348.

27   Stephen Westerholm, *Perspectives Old and New on Paul: The "Lutheran" Paul and His Critics* (Grand Rapids, MI: Eerdmans, 2004), 101.

28   E.P. Sanders, *Paul and Palestinian Judaism* (Philadelphia, PA: Fortress, 1977).

29   James D.G. Dunn, "The New Perspective on Paul," the Manson Memorial Lecture delivered in the University of Manchester on 4 November 1982; reprinted in his anthology, *The New Perspective on Paul* (Grand Rapids, MI: Eerdmans, 2008), 99–120.

30   Ibid.

31   Representative scholars of this view include Krister Stendahl, Mark Nanos, Peter Tomson, David Rudolph, Kathy Ehrensperger, Caroline Johnson Hodge, Mark Kinzer, and J. Brian Tucker.

32   For a history of this development and an argument for the latter translation, see Richard B. Hays, *The Faith of Jesus Christ: The Narrative Substructure of Galatians 3:1–4:11* (Grand Rapids, MI: Eerdmans, 2001).

33   D.A. Carson and Douglas J. Moo, *An Introduction to the New Testament* (Grand Rapids, MI: Zondervan, 2005), 408.

34   D.A. Carson, Peter T. O'Brien, and Mark Seifrid, eds., *Justification and Variegated Nomism*, 2 vols. (Grand Rapids, MI: Baker, 2001–2004).

35   Michael Bird, *The Saving Righteousness of God: Studies on Paul, Justification, and the New Perspective* (Eugene, OR: Wipf and Stock, 2007).

36   See, for example, David J. Rudolph, *A Jew to the Jews: Jewish Contours of Pauline Flexibility in 1 Corinthians 9:19–23* (Tübingen, Germany: Mohr Siebeck, 2011).

37 Mark Kinzer, "Final Destinies: Qualifications for Receiving an Eschatological Inheritance," *Kesher* 22 (Spring/Summer 2008): 42–78, 87–119.

38 Ibid.

39 Ibid.

40 Hays, *Faith of Jesus Christ*.

41 Sigve K. Tonstad, *Saving God's Reputation: The Theological Function of Pistis Iesou in the Cosmic Narratives of Revelation* (New York, NY: T&T Clark, 2007), 4.

42 Ibid.

43 As originally argued in his essay, "The New Perspective on Paul," which joins many of his later essays on the subject in the compendium *The New Perspective on Paul*.

44 Henri Blocher, "Justification of the Ungodly (*Sola Fide*): Theological Reflections," in Carson, O'Brien, and Seifrid, *Justification and Variegated Nomism: The Paradoxes of Paul* (Grand Rapids, MI: Baker, 2004), 495.

45 Rudolph, "Messianic Jews and Christian Theology: Restoring an Historical Voice to the Contemporary Discussion," *Pro Ecclesia* 14, no. 1 (2005): 58–84.

46 On the specific role of the church in the communication of this grace, a major difference between Catholics and Protestants still exists, but this is addressed in the next chapter.

47 "Protestants" from here on should be understood to mean Five *Solae* Protestants rather than those who may have, for example, renewed their communion with the Catholic Church or those who have never embraced all five *Solae* (i.e., Anglicans).

48 Solomon Schechter, *Some Aspects of Rabbinic Theology* (New York, NY: Macmillan, 1909), 18.

49 C.G. Montefiore, *Judaism and St. Paul: Two Essays* (London, England: Max Goschen, 1914), 74–75.

50 George Foot Moore, *The Age of the Tannaim* (vol. 3 of *Judaism in the First Centuries of the Christian Era*; Cambridge, MA: Harvard University Press, 1930), 151.

51 Carson, O'Brien, and Seifrid, *Justification and Variegated Nomism*.

52 Union of Messianic Jewish Congregations, "Statement of Faith," n.p. [cited 8 February 2014]. Online: http://www.umjc.org/faith-and-values/statement-of-faith.

53 See Charles Hodge, *II Corinthians* (*The Crossway Classic Commentaries*, ed. Alister McGrath and J.I. Packer; Wheaton, IL: Crossway, 1995), 53: "The law of Moses was, in the first place, a reenactment of the covenant of works ... When we look at this aspect, it is condemnation and death."

54 "Joint Declaration on the Doctrine of Justification," The Lutheran World Federation and the Catholic Church, 3.16, [cited 4 November 2014]. Online: http://www.vatican.va/roman_curia/pontifical_councils/chrstuni/documents/rc_pc_chrstuni_doc_31101999_cath-luth-joint-declaration_en.html.

55 Thomas Aquinas, *Summa Theologica* (trans. Fathers of the English Dominican Province; 5 vols.; Notre Dame, IN: Ave Maria, 1948), III, 61, i, ad. 2.

56 We explored in a previous chapter the fact that the salvation economy in Calvinism, in which there exists no totally volitional act on the part of the convert, is quite different and very much alien to a Messianic Jewish worldview.

57 D.T. Lancaster, *Torah Club: Chronicles of the Messiah* (Marshfield, MO: First Fruits of Zion, 2014), 1770–1771.

58 Among those scholars who have explored Protestantism's influence on the rise of Western democracy is Steve Bruce, "Did Protestantism Create Democracy?" *Democratization* 11, no. 4 (2004): 3–20.

59 Roger Williams, *The Bloudy Tenent of Persecution for Cause of Conscience, Discussed in a Conference between Truth and Peace* (1644). Besides the anti-Catholic polemic throughout, William's reliance on *solus Christus* is perhaps easiest to see when he states that "the means whereby the church may and should attain her ends are only ecclesiastical, which are chiefly five. First, setting up that form of church government only of which Christ hath given them a pattern in his Word. Secondly, acknowledging and admitting of *no lawgiver in the church but Christ and the publishing of His laws*" (emphasis added).

60 Theodore Alois Buckley, trans., *Canons and Decrees of the Sacred and Ecumenical Council of Trent* (London, England: Routledge, 1851), 213.

61 Bauckham, "James and the Jerusalem Community," 66–70.

62 Lancaster, *Torah Club: Chronicles of the Apostles* (Marshfield, MO: First Fruits of Zion, 2011), 167–168; Lancaster, *Torah Club: Chronicles of the Messiah*, 792–795.

63 The International Alliance of Messianic Congregations and Synagogues and the Union of Messianic Jewish Congregations.

64 Jan Jaben-Eilon, "Messianic Jewish Groups Claim Rapid Growth," n.p. [cited 4 November 2014]. Online: http://www.jewishjournal.com/religion/article/messianic_jewish_groups_claim_rapid_growth_20120612.

65 The Union of Messianic Jewish Congregations, the Messianic Jewish Rabbinical Council, and the Messianic Jewish Theological Institute.

66 The Hebrew and Aramaic Lexicon of the Old Testament (HALOT) divides definitions of *kavod* into two separate categories: theological and non-theological. Depending on one's perspective, this may solve or compound the problem; which kind of *kavod* is being referred to in Isaiah 42:8? HALOT indicates the former, but commentators are divided. Compare to Bruce Chilton, *The Glory of Israel: The Theology and Provenience of the Isaiah Targum* (Sheffield, England: JSOT, 1983), 75–76: "Glory is not the sole possession of God; men also can have glory or pretend to do so, although it is repeatedly asserted in the Targum that this is nothing compared to what God now possesses or will possess"; John Watts, *Isaiah 34–66* (vol. 25 of *Word Biblical Commentary*; Nashville, TN: Thomas Nelson, 1987), 2.119: "*My glory* refers to credit due to God for these events."

67 m.*Avot* 4.1.

68 m.*Avot* 4.6.

69 Aquinas, *Summa Theologica* II–II, 132, i.

70 See, for example, Stan Telchin, *Messianic Judaism Is Not Christianity: A Loving Call to Unity* (Grand Rapids, MI: Chosen, 2004).